Freedom by the Bay

Freedom by the Bay

The Boston Freedom Trail

by William G. Schofield

illustrated with photographs

RAND McNALLY & COMPANY

CHICAGO • NEW YORK • SAN FRANCISCO

Photographs reproduced courtesy of Greater Boston
Chamber of Commerce; John Hancock Mutual Life
Insurance Company as a joint public service with the
Freedom Trail Foundation of Boston, Mass.;
Massachusetts Department of Commerce and
Development, Division of Tourism; School of Public
Communication of Boston University (photographs
from former *Boston Herald Traveler* files); United
States Navy; University Photo Services of Boston
University

Jacket illustration: reproduction of Paul Revere's
engraving in collection of Paul Revere Life Insurance
Company

Library of Congress Cataloging in Publication Data

Schofield, William Greenough, 1909–
    Freedom by the Bay: the Boston Freedom Trail.
    1. Boston—History—Colonial period, ca. 1600–1775.
2. Boston—Description—1951–   3. Historic sites—
Boston. I. Title.   *4. US — History — Colonial period*
F73.4.S36   917.44'61'044   74-2006
ISBN 0-528-81941-0

By the Same Author

Ashes in the Wilderness
The Cat in the Convoy
Payoff in Black
The Deer Cry
Seek for a Hero
Sidewalk Statesman
Destroyers—60 Years
Treason Trail
Eastward the Convoys

Contents

Foreword • 11

Common Pleasures • 15

The Merrymount Caper • 25

Under the Golden Dome • 30

Bastion of Brimstone • 37

Grave Sites and Grave Slights • 46

From Cave to Culture • 54

Old South and Its Mouth • 65

Witch-Bane and Women's Lib • 73

Lion and Unicorn Country • 86

A "Cradle" Called Faneuil • 111

To the Old North End • 120

Paul Revere at Large • 126

Church for All People • 130

Copp's Hill Reflections • 136

View from the Hill • 142

Here Come the British! • 146

Index • 155

Freedom
by the Bay

for
Blanche

Foreword

WHEN JOHN B. HYNES was Mayor of Boston—back in 1951—
I proposed in a newspaper column that the city tie its historic sites
together in one sight-seeing package.

Tourists were going berserk in those days, bumbling around
and frothing at the mouth because they couldn't find what they
were looking for. It was not unusual for a safari trying to track
down Faneuil Hall to get lost in the tattoo shops and burlesque
dives of old Scollay Square. A family looking for Old North
Church might easily take a wrong turn and blunder headlong
into Boston Harbor. Nobody knew where anything was nor how
to get there if he did. It was chaos.

The obvious solution was to link the sites in numbered sequence
along a clearly marked and charted trail, so that a visitor might
follow the route from end to end without ever arriving at a
wrong door.

Mayor Hynes was enthusiastic about the idea. So was the
Chamber of Commerce. Thus the Freedom Trail was born. And
it made sense then, as it does now, that it followed precisely the
routes that hundreds of Boston colonials would have walked in
their daily 18th-century activities. For instance, Mrs. Joseph
Warren most certainly would have strolled across Boston Common

and down past King's Chapel on her way to buy codfish for the General at Faneuil Hall Market. Paul Revere, riding in from the North End, would surely have passed the Boston Stone and John Hancock's house of brick on his way to an anti-King George demonstration at Old South Meeting House. And it was directly along these routes that the major events took place that led to the birth of American freedom.

In a sense, I suppose I'm being racist when I undertake to write about freedom on the Bay shores of Massachusetts and coincide its beginnings with the struggles of the colonists. Such an approach ignores the fact that the Indians of Cape Cod, Plymouth, and Boston enjoyed freedom long before the colonists arrived.

But there was a difference. The Indians had freedom and were not, unfortunately, able to keep it. The Bay colonists longed for freedom and went all out to get it.

A great-great-great-etc.-grandfather of mine named William Nickerson, founder of the town of Chatham, was typical of the colonists who took a hand in effecting this change. And typical of some of the transactions of those days, he almost lost his shirt while stealing the shirts off the backs of the Indians. There's a point to my telling about Nickerson's case. He arrived in Massachusetts from Norwich, England, back in 1637. He brought with him his wife and four children. They settled in the Cape Cod town of Yarmouth in 1640. William immediately got into trouble with the courts, partly through a land-claim dispute with the influential Captain Myles Standish and partly through selling a rowboat to an Indian, which was a serious violation of colonial law. Thereupon, the record says, Nickerson "made offensive speeches against sundry of the town" and got slapped with a fistful of slander suits.

In 1656, he went looking for a more congenial neighborhood and wound up among the Indians of Chatham. That's where he swung his big real-estate coup and bought from the natives thousands of acres of the best land on Cape Cod. He paid off with 10 coats, 6 kettles, 12 axes, 12 hoes, 12 knives, 12 shillings, and one hat.

You'd think the Establishment would leave a man alone after a clever transaction like that; but no! The town of Yarmouth chased after him in the form of a tax collector named Tom

Howes, who at last overtook William in the woods and then hurried right back home complaining of singed ears. Thereupon the Plymouth Colony Court moved in and informed William he'd made an illegal purchase. He could keep 100 acres, they told him, but he'd have to pay a fine of five pounds per acre for all the rest of the land or hand it over to the court. Nickerson blew his stack, unloaded a barrage of curses, and rushed off to Boston, where he bought land in what is now the Roxbury section of the city.

He returned to Yarmouth in 1662, driving a cart that contained his wife and a barrel of rum. He promptly filed claim for a share of the profits from a gam of whales that had been trapped along the shore during his absence. This got him nowhere. So he rode off to Chatham again to plan a campaign of recovery and to practice his vengeful oratory among the trees and dunes.

To make the tale short, William spent the rest of his life in a sulfurous feud with the Plymouth authorities, trying to get back all the land they had plucked from him. He wrote insulting letters to almost every town official, and whenever he could spare the time, he'd show up at court sessions and public meetings intent on making a speech about the hideous injustice of the treatment he was getting. He even sailed to England a couple of times to cry out his complaints in Parliament.

His methods must have had some merit, because by 1689 he'd managed to get back 4,000 acres of his original purchase. It was a good chunk of land, but of course it didn't amount to a cornhill compared to his original stake. He was still fighting and fuming about the whole business when he died at the age of 86.

This is not a book about William Nickerson. I've told his story because this is a book about generations of men and women who were like him in most respects and who closely tended the growth of American freedom during the 17th and 18th centuries. History has presented them to us as puppets, as drab faceless people who were the epitome of moral righteousness and who derived their greatest enjoyment from hard work and long hours of prayer. They were not like that at all. They were doughty Englishmen, products of the strongest empire in the world. They were high-spirited, opinionated, tough, and proud. Like Nickerson, they were not above chicanery. Like Nickerson, their goals were big and bold. Like Nickerson, they would bellow and claw when they felt they were being pushed around. They were good fighters and wild dreamers. They dreamed of their right to freedom. They fought back when they thought they'd been wronged. They kept this up for 155 years before finally starting the Revolution.

Today in Boston, the stops along the Freedom Trail mark the sites where the dreams of these people became their descendants' deeds and where action gave birth to realities. To walk the Trail is to better understand just what the Bay colonists did and why they did it. They were the right kind of people for declaring an independence.

They are offered to the reader with respect, applause, and affection.

WILLIAM G. SCHOFIELD

Common Pleasures

FIVE BLOCKS southeast of Boston Common lies Boston's China-town. Thus, many Chinatown residents are alert to the fact that five blocks to the northwest of their neighborhood there are pigeons on the loose. Boston Common pigeons. Trustful, stupid birds that will waddle and flutter right up to a man and even perch on his forearm hoping to get a free meal. They are easy to catch.

So are the occasional Chinese who filter up from Chinatown's Beach Street or Tyler Street in the shadows of dawn, intent on snaring feathered food to be roasted, stewed, or barbecued. After they catch their pigeons, they in turn are usually caught by the Boston police, sometimes to be trundled off to court, sometimes simply to be escorted back home on a promise not to do it again—a promise to leave the pigeons alone, to enjoy Boston Common by all means and stroll in the shade of its name-tagged elm trees (*Ulmus americana, Ulmus brittanicus*) all they wish, but to remember that public pigeons are meant to be fed, not to be food.

The police cannot seem to understand why a Chinatown resi-dent would want to eat a pigeon. The poachers from China-town cannot understand why a fat, free-strutting bird, belonging to nobody in particular, should not be caught and cooked. But each side respects the other's feelings in the matter while asserting staunch disagreement. This is an example of freedom of opinion. It is an ancient and precious Boston heritage. Its roots are set deep in colonial history, for this is where freedom began and where it still waves a bright flag, hard by Boston Bay.

In Boston, as in any city that a man learns to love, the present is a fragile thing. The future, a mystery. But the past? There, now, is something dependable and worthy of a man's devotion, something to which he can give his mind and his heart. He can be lonely for it, weep over it, laugh at it or with it, get drunk on its spirits, overlook its sins, boast of its beauties, regret its unfulfilled dreams, and talk softly with it at intimate moments of midnight or noonday. And Boston responds, sometimes as a proud lady, sometimes as a wench. She can be either, depending upon how you go about making a pass at her.

You can meet her as a proud lady, for example, by strolling on Boston Common and pausing at the spot on Tremont Street where the red-brick pathway of the Freedom Trail begins. You ask yourself, why is the Trail here? Is it good for a city to cling so closely to its past? Is it healthy? Is it, perhaps, offensive to younger cities that were nothing but a collection of mangy tepees when Boston's constables were clubbing the Jesuits and cutting off the ears of Quakers?

Boston's response is yes, it's good to have a Freedom Trail, a path to follow along the streets and byways, walking in the footsteps of pugnacious rebels like James Otis and Samuel Adams and Paul Revere and all those other early New Englanders who took a close look at tyranny and said to hell with it.

The Trail is Boston's foremost tourist attraction. Nobody knows for certain just how many tens of millions of persons have followed its path since it came into being in 1951. It wanders from the Common to the State House; to "Brimstone Corner" and the Park Street Church; to Granary Burying Ground, where "Mother Goose" and Paul Revere and the parents of Benjamin Franklin are buried; to the Old South Meeting House, where patriots plotted the Boston Tea Party; to Faneuil Hall, the "Cradle of Liberty"; to the Old North Church and its lanterns— "two if by sea"—in the steeple; and to other historical landmarks in the birthplace of American freedom.

With this in mind then, you decide to walk the Trail and live for a time in the past. And that is what this book is all about.

But first you should elect to spend some thought on the Common itself and go back in history to a period long before the Revere-Adams-Otis days. This way, you come to realize that the spirit of freedom was alive on the shores of Boston Bay more than a century before the British Redcoats were reeling in and out of Boston's waterfront taverns.

The Freedom Trail of today is a brick-marked route that begins at the Common and weaves for a mile and a half among old streets and alleys and into the rooms and doorways where patriots once huddled to plot against a king. But the trail that led to Boston's freedom and to a nation's liberation began much earlier in New England's history.

So just where did it begin? You wonder about this as you walk the paths of Boston Common today, admiring the ancient headstones in the Central Burying Ground and only half-hearing the tinkling finger cymbals of the Hare Krishna dancers who have parked on the grass nearby for the afternoon.

Was colonist William Blackstone a free man when he owned this Common and grazed his cattle here back in the early 1630s? Certainly he was, in the sense that nobody had the right to yell at him, "Hey, Blackstone! Get your stupid cows off the grass!" Still, even then he must have sensed the stirring of some dark challenge to his personal freedom, for in 1635 he packed and left. He put his belongings into rough saddlebags and headed south, by way of what is now the black ghetto of Roxbury. Historians say he rode out of town on a white bull, but that seems a bit farfetched. On a cow, perhaps. Or an ox. But, a bull? One has the freedom to doubt this.

In any event, Blackstone vanished into the forest and kept on the move until in time he reached a spot, close to the border of Rhode Island, that is now occupied by the little town of Rehoboth. He settled there and lived contentedly on his corn, milk, cheese, beef, and johnnycakes until other early settlers moving inland from Plymouth and down from Boston had staked their land to within a mile or two of his property. Then he repacked his saddlebags and moved on again, this time westward to the lonely shore of Narragansett Bay. It would appear that Blackstone's idea of freedom was to shun all other people and to dwell in some place where he would not have to listen to any neighbor voicing unsolicited opinions about parliamentary politics or the societal rights of the Wampanoag Indians.

But just as one man covets the freedom not to listen, another cherishes the freedom to be heard. Today, as it has for decades past, Boston Common harbors a vociferous population of self-appointed preachers and orators. Usually they gather near the Parkman Bandstand, where freedom of speech enjoys all the respect and latitude it gets in London's Hyde Park. They harangue, heckle, filibuster, jeer, and jape. They flinch from no issue, spare nobody from insults. Some of them are living on their social security and civil service pensions; some are elderly professional men who enjoy spending their sunset days on a park bench without having to worry about their dignity; some are retired office clerks.

Whatever their backgrounds or their ages, they splay forth their verbal attacks like shotgun blasts, sometimes pelting bishops, sometimes abortionists, sometimes senators, sometimes the Chinese cooks who ambush and snare the pigeons, sometimes the police who ambush and snare the cooks. In short, they're free to say whatever they wish to say, and they're usually tolerant enough to grant dissenters equal freedom.

"If Gibbon were here, he'd bewail the decline and fall of American patriotism!" cries the ranting voice from the bandstand.

"If Gibbon were here, he'd cite you as an example!" shouts a voice from the crowd.

Applause.

Boston bought the Common land from William Blackstone for 30 pounds in 1634 when the Town Fathers decided they needed an open grassy reservation for the feeding of cattle and the training of militia.

Blackstone's 48-acre tract was considered ideal for both purposes, and it still is. To this day, as a matter of fact, any taxpayer is free to drive his cows there and let them graze. To this day also, the Ancient and Honorable Artillery Company of Massachusetts still meets annually on the Common to choose its officers by drumhead election and to fire its cannon in celebration of the event. The "Ancients," incidentally, were chartered in 1638 and claim to be the oldest military organization in the western hemisphere; and although they have never fought in any war as a unit, they still perform with enthusiasm their annual "tour of duty"—in such potential "trouble spots" as Paris, Rome, Vienna, London, Bermuda. But they always return to the Common.

The Common was little more than a boggy meadow cluttered with thickets when Blackstone first set foot on it in 1625. Indians in some time past had named the area Shawmut and then had abandoned most of it to the animals that prowled its hummocks and the fish that occasionally flipped onto its shores.

But that was just the sort of seclusion that Blackstone had been looking for. He had journeyed from England to Salem and then had pushed south through dark forest in search of a place where he'd be free from the clattering tongues of neighbors and especially from the obtrusive ministers of church sects. He just wanted to be left alone. And Shawmut's wooded shore, later to become Boston Common, provided exactly the kind of isolation he had been seeking.

Many years later, Oliver Wendell Holmes wrote a poem that evoked a picture of the arrival scene as it must have been:

> All overgrown with bush and fern,
>   And straggling clumps of tangled trees,
> With trunks that lean and boughs that turn,
>   Bent eastward by the mastering breeze,—
> With spongy bogs that drip and fill
>   A yellow pond with muddy rain,
> Beneath the shaggy southern hill
>   Lies wet and low the Shawmut plain.
> And hark! the trodden branches crack;
>   A crow flaps off with startled scream;
> A straying woodchuck canters back;
>   A bittern rises from the stream;
> Leaps from its lair a frightened deer;
>   An otter plunges in the pool,—
> Here comes old Shawmut's pioneer,
>   The parson on his brindled bull.

Not that Blackstone himself was a parson; he was, rather, a dedicated hermit. However, the pioneers who shortly followed him to the boggy meadow not only included professional parsons but also would, in time, create their own brand of minister whenever there was a shortage. So if legend is correct, Blackstone soon departed in the same manner in which he'd arrived and for largely the same reasons.

For several years after the Town Fathers bought the Common land, they seemed to have forgotten what they had bought it for. It didn't exactly fall into disuse; rather, it seemed destined to become the Town Dump. There were so many people using it for an outdoor disposal unit that the authorities were forced to pass a law in 1652 making it a criminal offense to treat the Common as an abattoir waste pile. The official order enacted that year forbade using the Common as a dumping ground for "entrails of beasts or fowls, or garbage or carrion, or dead dogs or cats, or any other dead beast or stinking thing."

With that taken care of, the Common quickly recovered its good health and was witness to a fascinating succession of events that included the strangling of pirates, the garroting of Quakers, the hanging of witches, the stoning of Catholics, the baiting of bears, the fighting of duels, the beating of slaves, the caging of Sabbath breakers, and the drenching of sinners by means of a ducking stool overhanging Frog Pond, which today contains no frogs.

This sequence of excitements, which began to develop immediately, shows clearly how extreme were the passions and the pleasures of the people who flocked to the Bay Colony under the banner of Puritanism. Their convictions as a whole were either black or white and rarely gray. They were violent or benign, God-fearing or cynical, avaricious or generous, and seldom anything in between.

The historian Samuel Eliot Morison, in defining Puritanism in his work *The Puritan Pronaos,* has described it as:

"A party in the Church of England that arose in Elizabeth's reign with the purpose of carrying out the Protestant reformation to its logical conclusion, to base the English Church both in doctrine and discipline on the firm foundation of Sacred Scripture; or in the words of Cartwright, to restore the primitive, apostolic church 'pure and unspotted' by human accretions or inventions. Religion should permeate every phase of living. Man belonged to God alone: his only purpose in life was to enhance God's glory and do God's will, and every variety of human activity, every sort of human conduct, presumably unpleasing to God, must be discouraged if not suppressed."

But there were many individuals in the early Bay Colony of the Puritans, and in the Pilgrims' neighboring Plymouth Colony as well, who took exception to religious guidelines; actually many who arrived in New England came solely in search of adventure and profit and cared not a hoot about the nourishing of a "pure and unspotted" church. Some 20,000 people came from England to the Bay Colony in less than ten years, and it was hardly to be expected that they would all be dedicated to the principles of religious freedom. Some, of course, were so fanatically dedicated that they were ready to persecute to the point of death any and all dissenters, thereby creating in New England a religious climate every bit as harsh as the one they had fled; but others merely paid lip service to religion, putting up with its rigidities in order to settle in New England and turn a financial profit.

To begin with, they could argue that the original Bay area settlement at Gloucester had been established in 1623 under Thomas Gardner and John Tilley not for religious purposes but solely to make money in the fishing industry for an English firm known as the Dorchester Company of Adventurers. The settlement at Naumkeag (which became Salem in 1629) was established in 1626 by Roger Conant only because the Gloucester fishing venture turned out to be a financial dud. The legal authority for both the Gloucester and Salem settlements was the patents granted to the Reverend John White of Dorchester, England, and his associates for the advancement of economic development. John Endicott, who was later to become a governor of the Massachusetts Bay Colony, was sent to Salem in the ship *Abigail* in 1628 not because he knew his Bible well but because the New England Company, which succeeded the Dorchester Company, considered him an astute businessman who could straighten out their financial troubles. It's true that Endicott was also commissioned to make the Gospel known to the Indians and that he was promised a "plentiful provision of godly ministers" to help with this project; but it was made clear that his prime mission was to make money for the company from lumber, fish, and furs and from farming and any other way he could turn a shilling.

Not until 1630, when John Winthrop, who had been elected governor of the Massachusetts Bay Colony when it was chartered the previous year, arrived with a thousand settlers in a convoy of ships, did religion have its real impact on the Bay Colony. Puritanism now became the dominant force of life—political as well as religious —in the Boston area, assuring the independence of the newly established Congregational Church.

Even then, Winthrop was a bit hesitant to challenge the Church of England to a showdown on the principles of religious freedom. While eager to see the Congregational Church flourish, he nevertheless called upon all the people of England to "take notice of the principals and body of our Company, as those who esteem it our honor to call the Church of England, from whence we rise, our dear mother; and cannot part from our native country, where she specially resideth, without much sadness of heart and many tears in our eyes, ever acknowledging that such hope and part as we have obtained in the common salvation we have received in her bosom, and sucked it from her breasts.

"We leave it not, therefore, as loathing that milk wherewith we were nourished there; but, blessing God for the parentage and education, as members of the same body, shall always rejoice in her good, and unfeignedly grieve for any sorrow that shall ever betide her, and while we have breath, sincerely desire and endeavor the continuance and abundance of her welfare, with the enlargement of her bounds in the Kingdom of Christ Jesus."

Such a weighty declaration as this would lead one to believe that Winthrop was a stern and dour sort of individual, and for the most part, that has been his picture in history. But excerpts from the letters he sent from Boston to his wife back in England show him in another light: "And now, my sweet soul . . . . So I kiss my sweet wife and rest . . . . I shall yet again see thy sweet face, that lovely countenance that I have so much delighted in . . . . I take thee in my arms, and kiss and embrace you." Obviously he cared for other things in life besides the creating of Congregational ministers.

In any event, such were the forces in collision in Boston at the time the Common was established: cruelty and mercy, praying and profiteering, bigotry and benevolence.

The Common soon became a popular spot for hangings. Marmaduke Stevenson and William Robinson, Quakers who had been exiled and defied the law by returning to Boston, were strung up there on October 27, 1659. The Quaker Mary Dyer accompanied them on their journey to the gallows, walking along between them, holding their hands, and tossing her head at the catcalls from the crowd. One year later, she too was hanged, in the same place and for the same offense. And in 1661, another Quaker, William Leddra, swung from a noose.

Of the duels that were fought on the Common grass, some were insignificant, like the one in 1718 between Captain Thomas Smart and John Boydell. They fought over some point of honor, long since lost in history; and after all their thrashings and slashings were ended, they suffered only minor wounds and were jailed for their actions. But other duels were tragic, as was the fight some ten years later between Benjamin Woodbridge and Henry Phillips. Both were popular young men, well-known and highly respected, the sons of good families. Their quarrel began in a tavern, either over a game of cards or over a love rivalry—nobody is quite sure which. Whatever, they adjourned to the Common and fought it out with short swords, flailing away at each other until finally Phillips ran his opponent through the heart and left him on the ground to die. With the aid of his cousin, the respected merchant Peter Faneuil, Phillips was spirited aboard a British ship and fled to exile in France, where he died of loneliness and a broken heart.

But the Common was used for many purposes besides executions and duels. There were gay times as well. For instance, it was a popular place for outdoor spinning and weaving; on one day in 1753, there were 300 women and men all working on the Common at the same time, with looms and wheels and shuttles all whirling and clattering in the breeze.

And the year 1770 might well be called the Barbecue Year. The popular pastime then was to build huge fires and roast oxen for the poor. And through the years following, there were Punch and Judy shows, carnivals with cake tents and candy tents, baseball and football, coasting and kite flying, and many visits by young lovers to the Wishing Stone near Beacon Hill. There was always something doing on the Common.

One of the days worth recalling was the occasion in 1834 when President Andrew Jackson and Vice-President Martin Van Buren were on hand to review troops of the Massachusetts Militia. Upon their arrival, they were greeted with a tremendous roar of cannon fire, which so frightened Van Buren's horse that the animal panicked and went galloping across the meadow, hurling himself against an iron fence where he got enmeshed in the bars and pinned Van Buren into helpless immobility.

"Where's the vice-president?" said Jackson, halfway through the ceremony. "Wait, I see him—on the fence as usual."

Today, of course, the Common is a far different sweep of land than it was in the beginning. If Blackstone could return, he would never recognize the place. Where the sea lapped the shore, there is now the busy rush of traffic along Charles Street. Where trees were tangled, there are now lovely rolling knolls and manicured lawns. Where settlers buried their dead and left dueling victims to lie with a stake through the heart, there is now a huge underground garage. Where Blackstone's cows huddled against wintry winds, there is now an annual Christmas pageantry display.

Nobody grazes his cows on the Common anymore. One of the last to do so was Ralph Waldo Emerson; his mother made him do it.

The Merrymount Caper

PROBABLY AT NO TIME in the early days of Plymouth Colony and the Bay Colony did the scruples of religion and the high spirits of free living get into a more basic clash than in the brief life of the Merrymount settlement.

This fascinating little village was the original bayside center of fun and games for colonial cutups. It never achieved the historic fame of Boston Common, but during its short span of action it produced more than its share of turmoil and excitement. Before it was forced out of business, it had both Governor John Endicott of the Bay Colony and Governor William Bradford of Plymouth Colony rushing troops to the scene to put down a homegrown revolution of fun, free sex, and frivolity.

Merrymount—somewhat in the nature of a year-round New Orleans Mardi Gras, Munich Oktoberfest, and Sicilian Carnevale rolled into one—was situated on an attractive slope overlooking the bay some eight miles south of Boston in what is now the town of Wollaston.

The settlement had its beginnings in 1625 when a company of some 40 men, led by one Captain Wollaston, arrived from England and tramped north from Plymouth about 28 miles to settle down and establish a trading post.

Captain Wollaston soon had second thoughts about the venture; he sailed away to Virginia and into historical oblivion. Remaining behind as leader, however, was one who signed himself "Thomas Morton, Gent." And Morton was probably the liveliest, merriest, swingiest "Gent" who ever set foot in the Bay Colony.

One history book—*The Story of Massachusetts,* Vol. I by Marsh and Clark—refers to him as "a boisterous creature with a sincere appreciation of the beauty of the fields and woods and waters which must have made Boston Bay one of the most pleasant places on the face of the earth."

That scarcely tells the story. It says nothing of his appreciation for the joys of guzzling rum, dancing naked in the moonlight, and rolling in the daisies with young Indian maidens.

Back in London, Thomas Morton, Gent., had been a well-educated lawyer with an avidity for wine, women, song, and the writing of lurid poetry. Following the discovery of an awesome shortage in the funds of one of his clients' estates, he left England for Plymouth. Since there was little opportunity to practice law in the Bay Colony and no profitable estates on which to work, he decided to exercise his other talents. It was a remarkable instance of the right man being in the right place at just the right moment.

Captain Wollaston had scarcely put the bayside scene behind him before Morton changed the name of the settlement from Mount Wollaston to Ma-re Mount, meaning Mountain by the Sea. To the somber Pilgrims in nearby Plymouth, the name sounded like Merrymount; they referred to it as such, with much raising of eyebrows and clucking of tongues about the sin of making merry in the midst of hard times.

Eventually the Pilgrims sent a small group of fact-finding observers to Morton's bailiwick to learn just what was going on. Having seen and sampled some of the joys of Merrymount, several observers decided to stay there and share in the fun. Those who returned to Plymouth, however, carried back tales of such shocking behavior that Governor Bradford, the Pilgrims' chief chronicler, promptly inscribed in his journal the worst invectives he could think of to pin down Morton, Gent., for the benefit of future historians.

"Pettifogger!" Bradford railed. "The lord of misrule, tending to lasciviousness. An instrument of mischief!"

And when it was officially confirmed that Morton had indeed named his settlement something that sounded like "Merrymount," Bradford bitterly deplored the act for the records:

"After this," he fumed, "they fell to great licentiousness and led to a dissolute life, pouring out themselves into all profaneness . . . . They also set up a maypole, drinking and dancing about it many days together, inviting the Indian women for their consorts, dancing and frisking together like so many fairies, or furies rather; and worse practices. As if they had anew revived and celebrated the feasts of the Roman Goddess Flora, or the beastly practices of the mad Bacchanalians."

Morton, who by now was calling himself "Mine Host of Ma-re Mount," found Bradford's tantrums highly amusing. In reply to the name-calling, he dubbed Bradford "Rhadamant," choosing the name of a mythical judge of the underworld of whom Bradford probably never had heard.

Bradford threatened to send the diminutive Captain Myles Standish to Merrymount with a company of Plymouth soldiers under orders to destroy the place. Morton's reply derided Standish as "Captain Shrimp" and in effect dared him to try.

Meanwhile, "Mine Host" was still writing lurid poems and seeing to it that they were recited and heard in the streets of Plymouth. He wrote, for example:

> Give to the nymph that's free from scorn
> No Irish stuff nor Scotch o'erworn.
> Lasses in beaver coats, come away,
> Ye shall be welcome to us night and day.
>
> Then drink and be merry, merry, merry boys,
> Let all your delight be in Hymen's joys;
> Io! to Hymen, now the day is come,
> About the merry Maypole take a room.

Bradford was furious. But all his bristling and ranting had no effect on Morton's Bacchic carousing.

By 1628, various restless men from Boston and Plymouth alike were finding their way to Merrymount, pushing through the woods and along the shore to join the band of merrymakers. Meanwhile,

Morton's business with the Indians was flourishing, for he was acquiring a profitable stockpile of their beaver skins, trading for these with firewater and guns.

"And first he taught them how to use them [the guns]," Bradford moaned in his chronicle, "to charge and discharge, and what proportion of powder to give the piece . . . and what shot to use for fowl and what for deer . . . . O, the horribleness of this villainy!"

Obviously, from Bradford's point of view, something had to be done to keep Morton's honky-tonk zone from spreading. The Plymouth Fathers forthwith deputized Myles Standish to lead a vice squad of soldiers to Merrymount "to cleanse the place and make it decent."

The battle that followed seems to have had overtones of a comic-opera barroom brawl or a Laurel and Hardy debacle. History fails to determine which side was drunker, the followers of Thomas Morton, Gent., or those of Captain Shrimp. Perhaps in their hangovers, none of the combatants could clearly remember.

In Bradford's version of the fray, Morton and his merry men locked themselves and their jugs inside their Merrymount block-house and proceeded to get themselves so thoroughly soused they could scarcely lift their guns, let alone shoot straight. Bradford maintained that the merrymakers were captured without a shot being fired and that the only injury of the day was to one of Morton's men who was "so drunk that he ran his own nose upon the point of a sword . . . but lost but a little of his hot blood."

As for Morton, Bradford wrote, "Himself with a carbine, over-charged and almost half filled with powder and shot, had thought to have shot Captain Standish; but he [Standish] stepped to him and put by his piece and took him."

Morton's version of the fight was somewhat different. He maintained that Standish and his soldiers, having laid siege to the blockhouse, spent the day hitting the bottle; they finally got so rum-soaked that they passed out en masse, whereupon the merrymakers quietly stole away, stepping gingerly around the sodden sleepers.

"Their grand leader, Captain Shrimp, took on most furiously," Morton wrote, "and tore his clothes for anger to see the empty nest and their bird gone."

However that may be, the "bird" did not get very far. He was chased into the woods, quickly collared by Standish, and then bundled off to Plymouth to be shipped back to England. Meanwhile, Governor Endicott in Boston, hearing of the Merrymount fracas, rounded up a force of troops and set out for the scene himself.

All the action was over by the time Endicott arrived since he was only three months late, so the Bay Colony Governor had to content himself with chopping down Morton's 80-foot maypole and berating the disgruntled Indians on the evils of their ways.

So ended Merrymount.

But not Morton. He was too slick to be dismissed that easily. A year after the battle of the maypole, one Isaac Allerton arrived in Plymouth from England to pay an official business visit to the Pilgrims and establish new trade relations. He brought with him his secretary—who turned out to be none other than "Mine Host" himself, still writing poetry and singing the joys of Hymen.

"He not only brought him over," spluttered the indignant Bradford, "but to the town [itself] and lodged him at his own house . . . till he was caused to pack him away."

Morton, given his walking papers, thereupon returned to what remained of Merrymount, hoping to revive old dealings with Indian maidens and renew his beaverskin affairs. He was shortly intercepted there by the Puritans of Boston and sent sailing off to England once again.

In the autumn of 1643, the persistent Morton came back one more time to Plymouth. On this occasion, however, he was described by Edward Winslow of the Pilgrim band as being a changed and chastened man, even "content to drink water."

The Pilgrims were convinced that he was too far gone to cause further trouble, and so they allowed him to stay the winter. With the coming of spring, though, they hustled him off to Maine. He died there in 1646. And it is said that when the news reached Plymouth, the whole town celebrated with an extra and spontaneous Thanksgiving Day.

Whatever his failings, Thomas Morton, Gent., was unquestionably America's pioneer advocate of life, liberty, the pursuit of happiness, and doing your own thing. If nothing else, he introduced to the New World a brand of freedom and chicanery that was destined to flourish for centuries.

Under the Golden Dome

ATOP BOSTON'S BEACON HILL, on land which once belonged to John Hancock, there is a "new" Massachusetts State House; "new" because it was begun in 1795.

It is quite magnificent in its way, with its graceful golden dome looking down upon Boston Common in one direction, up the Charles River in another, northwestward across the river to Cambridge, and eastward out toward Boston Bay and the sea beyond.

It was designed so by the architectural genius Charles Bulfinch, who was assured by the state legislature (the General Court) that money was no object—that he could virtually write his own check for the cost of his commission, provided he produced a building of exquisite taste and beauty. For a time, this openhanded treatment of public funds caused the taxpayers to cry out in angry indignation and threaten to throw the entire state government out of office and into prison. But nothing came of the uproar. Governor Samuel Adams and Paul Revere calmly went ahead with plans for the laying of the cornerstone, and when the building was completed three years later, it had cost the taxpayers exactly $133,333.33.

Today it could not be replaced for millions. In fact, much of it, such as the imported Siena marble in the Hall of Flags, is irreplaceable. Italy no longer has such marble to send abroad.

Although it tops Beacon Hill and originally overlooked all of Boston, the State House still is not as high as it might have been. Until the mid-1700s, Beacon Hill actually consisted of three peaks, each with two names. There was Beacon Hill, also known as Sentry Hill (and The Hill by Bostonians today); there were two lesser peaks, Cotton Hill, alias Pemberton Hill, and Mount Vernon, also known as Mount Whoredom. Back about 1640, the Hill was crowned not by buildings but by a fire-fed beacon consisting of a 65-foot-tall pole topped by a flame pot. The iron pot was designed to flare alarm signals to the surrounding countryside and to ships at sea in case of invasion. After a century or so had passed and no invaders had arrived, the beacon was torn down. So was much of Beacon Hill itself.

Beacon Hill, Fort Hill, and Copp's Hill were the three hills that gave Boston its first English name—Trimountain (or Tri-mountane). Between 1755 and 1835, land-hungry Bostonians cut 110 feet off the top slopes of Beacon Hill and leveled its other two peaks, as well as all of Fort Hill, completely. They dumped the dirt and gravel into the Charles River, Boston Harbor, and the Back Bay tidal marshes to extend the city's waterfront and improve its tax base. Trimountain lives on, but only in terms of landfill and in the name of Tremont Street.

The "new" State House atop the Hill is the second stop on the Freedom Trail (the Old State House being the 11th), and as such, the Bulfinch masterpiece commands the early attention of tourists visiting Boston.

Occasionally some critic will argue that the State House should never have been included in the Freedom Trail at all, since it was not in existence at the time the colonists rose against King George III. However, since Beacon Hill most certainly was in existence and John Hancock's home was there, it seems not at all inappropriate for history buffs today to trudge up the slope from Boston Common to the top of a hill that looked down upon so many of the early scenes in the fight for freedom.

The renowned Oliver Wendell Holmes is said to have described his beloved Boston as the "Hub of the Universe." That report is not accurate. What Holmes asserted, when writing *The Autocrat of the Breakfast Table,* was that the "Boston State House is the hub of the solar system."

However that may be, the State House is at least a fascinating history museum, containing such relics as the first Yankee musket to be fired in the Revolution, the first British firing piece to be captured by the Yankees (at Concord), Bradford's history *Of Plimoth Plantation* (in which he excoriates Morton and Merrymount), hundreds of bullet-torn and bloodstained battle flags, the Charter of the Massachusetts Bay Company of 1629, the Constitution of 1780 (still in effect today), cannon captured from the British in the War of 1812, and literally thousands of other interesting historic artifacts.

The day of the State House cornerstone laying in 1795 fell appropriately enough on the Fourth of July. The cornerstone was hauled into position by 15 white horses, representing the 13 original states plus two latecomers, Vermont and Kentucky. A silver plate that had been wrought by Paul Revere and inscribed with the names of all those taking part in the ceremony was placed in position to be permanently sealed beneath the stone.

There had been some question as to whether Governor Sam Adams would be able to attend the affair. He was only 73 years old, but he had grown almost helplessly enfeebled as a result of the demanding sort of life he had led, what with arguing and fighting and drinking and harassing the Redcoats; in fact, two years earlier, he had been too weak to walk in the funeral procession of his old friend John Hancock. However, Adams not only arrived to preside at the ceremony but also gave a memorable address in dedicating the cornerstone.

May the building that will rise above it, he said, "remain, permanent as the enduring mountains; may the principles of our excellent Constitution, founded in Nature and in the Rights of Man, be ably defended here."

Another colorful portion of the ceremony that day consisted of Paul Revere at the head of a column of marching Masons, taking part as Grand Master of the Grand Lodge of Massachusetts and making a formal speech most appropriate to the occasion. (Revere must have made scores of speeches, but this is the only one that remains preserved.)

"Worshipful brethren," he said, "I congratulate you on this auspicious day when the Arts and Sciences are establishing themselves among us in our happy country, a country distinguished from the rest of the world by being a government of laws, where liberty has found a safe and secure abode, and where her sons are determined to support and protect her."

Revere, incidentally, seems to have made something of a profitable sideline out of his association with the State House. He created much of the building's ornate metalwork as well as its huge chandeliers, which were lowered twice a day and filled with illuminating whale oil. He arranged for his son-in-law, Amos Lincoln, to be appointed Master Builder in overall charge of construction. And when the building was completed in 1798, Revere became its first custodian.

In addition, Revere was back on the scene in 1802 when the great wooden dome was beginning to show signs of early rot. The legislators, worried over the possibility of a collapse on their heads, approved an appropriation of $4,000 to pay for 6,000 feet of copper sheathing for the dome. The contract, of course, went to Revere & Son and to the copper mill he had recently established in nearby Canton with the help of a federal subsidy.

As for Charles Bulfinch, his design of the State House was to bring him even greater commissions. The young Harvard graduate was scarcely 32 years old at the time of the cornerstone laying, but it was acknowledged by the best architectural authorities of the day that even if he never created another design, he would enjoy lasting fame for the superb structure on Beacon Hill. He did not stop there, however, but later went to Washington at the request of President James Monroe to rebuild the National Capitol and restore what the British had burned in 1814.

In 1861, Governor Nathaniel Banks urged that the State House dome be gilded; but not until 1874 was gold leaf actually applied. This in turn was covered with gray paint during the blackout days of World War II to thwart any German bombers that might arrive over Boston; but within two years after the war, the dome was given a new covering of 23½-karat gold leaf. And so it gleams today.

Strange occupants and strange events have enlivened the lobbies and corridors beneath the dome as the years moved along. Illegal bookmaking rings have thrived and been crushed. Politicians have staged bloody fistfights in the hallways and rest rooms. Sex parties have been disclosed and been hushed. Enraged lawmakers have been known to smash down solid-oak office doors with crowbars and axes to get at the necks of their opponents. And a few years ago, somebody in the State Surgeon General's office opened a file drawer that hadn't been touched in decades and discovered a tremendous cache of uncut heroin, morphine, and opium.

And then too there have been occasions when wild animals decided to move in and enjoy the surroundings. Skunks have come and gone. So have woodchucks and raccoons. So have frogs from the Charles River. At one time not long ago, a mink was in residence, scuttling back and forth and disrupting legislative committee meetings until it was finally trapped and turned over to the SPCA. And in 1951, a bushy-tailed silver fox staked out an apartment claim among the basement steam pipes; it was seen frequently at night, trotting through the Hall of Flags, gamboling among the seats of the Senate chamber, occupying the Governor's office, and running hither and yon, until finally it was stalked to its cellar lair and subdued by liberal squirtings of ammonia.

Among the less-active representatives of wildlife in the State House is the Sacred Cod of Massachusetts. This five-foot pinewood replica of a codfish, symbol of Massachusetts' ties with the sea and the fishing industry, was originally on view in the Old State House. Usually it hangs suspended over the center gallery in the chamber of the House of Representatives, except when it becomes a victim of codnappings. These take place unpredictably—whenever the codnappers, who are usually university students, take a liking to the wooden fish and decide to give it a new home in some such place as Harvard Yard. Up to now, the Sacred Cod has always been successfully retrieved and replaced, to hang once again above the heads of the state representatives.

Even apart from the State House, Beacon Hill today still stands as a vibrant symbol of colonial tradition and of Boston's unquenchable urge for independence. And it is a place of beauty as well, with its narrow lanes, cobbled streets, red-brick sidewalks, curbside gas lamps, walled gardens, brass door knockers, and purple windowpanes.

The purple windows, incidentally, are not a sign of special social status but are the result of a mistake made by some early-19th-century English glassmaker. When a cargo of his windowpanes arrived at Boston and were found to be tinted rather than clear, the Beacon Hill residents were delighted with the effect and prompt-ly placed orders for more of the same. Some Hillites are still buying them.

Throughout the years, the Hill has been home for many of Boston's most distinguished families, most skilled artists, most tal-ented statesmen, most learned scholars, and most astute businessmen, as well as for Bohemians, young-marrieds, and social freaks. Its better-known residents have included such remarkable persons as Daniel Webster, Louis Brandeis, Julia Ward Howe, Edwin Booth, Nathaniel Hawthorne, Louisa May Alcott, John Singer Sargent, Oliver Wendell Holmes, Samuel Eliot Morison, and Henry James, who once described the Hill's Mount Vernon Street as "the only respectable street in America."

The Hill has been both a suburb of the city and a village within the heart of the city. Back in the 1790s, a pharmacist named John Joy built a house where Beacon Street and Joy Street now in-tersect because he wanted "a home in the country." Some years later, a couple built a house on the Hill, on Cedar Lane, because they wanted to "move back to town"—all the way from nearby Marlborough Street.

The Hill and its people can be very stuffy in attitude, as was demonstrated a few years ago when fire broke out in the Brahmin-laced Somerset Club on Beacon Street; the fire fighters on arrival were ordered to remove themselves from the front door and go around to the service entrance. It can also be very small-townish and neighborly, as was demonstrated by Judge Frederick Pickering Cabot, who used to sell eggs from his suburban farm, delivering them personally to his Beacon Hill customers. The wealthy judge would make his daily rounds on foot before going along to conduct his duties in court. Judge Cabot was also president of the Boston Symphony Orchestra's Board of Trustees. When he stepped on stage at an afternoon concert in Symphony Hall one Friday, a little girl in the audience led everybody else in enthusiastic applause. "That's our egg man!" she cried to those around her.

Another quaint story among the many that apply to the Hill tells of the evening when Oliver Wendell Holmes was walking home up the slope of Mount Vernon Street and happened to notice a little boy trying frantically to grope high enough to reach the brass knocker on a tall front door. Holmes considerately stepped up to the boy's side, grabbed the door knocker, gave it several loud bangs, and said, "There you are, son. How's that?"

"Great!" said the youngster. "Now run like hell!"

Such is life among the narrow Hill streets with their ancient brick sidewalks—which nearly lost their bricks in 1947. That was the year the city decided to rip up the bricks and repave the walkways with cement. When the work crews arrived to begin the job, they found hundreds of Hill residents sitting stubbornly on their bricked paths and refusing to move. The city quietly dropped its plans, and the bricks remained in place.

Tourists who follow the Freedom Trail and explore the Hill and take the trouble to visit the State House with its golden dome, should be apprised of the fact that there is another "Golden Dome" just a short distance down Beacon Hill, about a block from the State House steps. This second "Golden Dome" happens to be a pub that is highly popular with the legislators, because of the good quality of its drinks and the convenience of its location; it's easy for any bored lawmaker to slip away from his legislative duties and hurry downhill for two or three quick drinks at the nearby bar, and he'll never be missed.

At any time, however, when the pub is packed with politicians taking a martini break, it is not unlikely that a messenger from the State House will rush panting through the front door and yell, "Roll call vote!" This will be the signal for everyone to gulp his drink and dash hurriedly back up the hill to get to his seat in the legislature.

Visitors should beware of this. It can be quite a stampede. Anybody trying to buck the onrush doesn't stand a chance.

Bastion of Brimstone

ON LEAVING the State House, and sidestepping any uphill rush by swiggers from the Golden Dome tavern, a Freedom Trail follower will cross Beacon Street and start strolling down the pleasant slope of Park Street. This path leads past the haughty quarters of the Union Club, where none but the true Boston blueblood may relax over his tiffin, and on past the Paulist Fathers Center and Chapel, where muffled shouts from within may indicate the seething of fresh controversy over recent pronouncements from the Vatican; like the colonial Bostonians before them, the Paulists have strong opinions of their own and a reputation for being outspoken.

But that's all right; in fact, it fits well with the historic atmosphere of the neighborhood, for here at the foot of the slope where Park Street meets Tremont Street, is Boston's "Brimstone Corner," site of the old, beautiful, and staunchly independent Park Street Church.

No one today is quite certain how the Corner first acquired its nickname. However, there are three theories on the subject, and anybody who is interested has full freedom to choose the one he likes. But whichever of the three versions he selects, he can be sure that the subscribers to the other two will be quick to tell him he's wrong.

One school of advocates maintains that Brimstone Corner was so named because brimstone for the making of gunpowder during the War of 1812 was stored there in an underground crypt of the Park Street Church. This theory combines historical fact with logic.

A second school insists that the corner was so named because of the sulfurous, thunderbolt sermons that were hurled at the heads of Bostonians by early fire-and-brimstone preachers in the church. Park Street parishioners tend to reject this belief.

A third explanation is that the devil arrived in Boston one night, staggered into the church, and never came out.

Regardless of all this, the corner was famous as the site of the Park Street Church before it was famous for any association with brimstone.

The Church was founded in 1809 by 30 Congregationalist members of the Old South Church, who found themselves being reduced to a minority group by a swell of citywide enthusiasm for Unitarian teachings. Obviously, if they wanted to maintain their free speech and peace of mind, they would have to set up a new church of their own. Accordingly they chose a site that overlooked Boston Common in one direction and the old town Granary and Burying Ground in another. Then they commissioned architect Peter Banner to design for them "the sightliest building in the country."

Banner based his ideas for the design on Christopher Wren's classic concept for St. Bride's in London, which casts the shadow of its graceful 217-foot spire down upon Fleet Street. The result of Banner's work was a true masterpiece of grace and beauty, which Henry James once inadequately described as "the most interesting mass of brick and mortar in America." It is all of that and much more, lending a presence of lovely serenity to one of the busiest street corners in the city.

Since its completion in 1810, the Park Street Church has always been active in the vanguard of movements for the reform and betterment of mankind as visualized and interpreted by its membership. In the year of its opening, it became the organizing site for the American Board of Commissioners for Foreign Missions; in 1815, for the American Education Society; in 1824, the Prison Reform Society; in 1826, the American Missionary Association and the American Temperance Society.

These were not its only firsts. On July 4, 1829, 24-year-old William Lloyd Garrison stood up in the Park Street Church pulpit and thundered out his first public address in condemnation of slavery. "I will be heard!" he cried, and he was. And on July 4th two years later, at a children's holiday party in the church, the youngsters began singing a song that began with the words *"My country, 'tis of thee,"* and the anthem "America" was born.

The fact that a religious dispute led to the founding of the Park Street Church was fully in keeping with the traditions that had been passed along by the fractious settlers of the Bay Colony. Religion to them was more than a source of spiritual comfort; it was also an excuse for bitter argument and petty tyrannies.

The Puritan clergymen of early colonial days were stern and gloomy believers in a God of Vengeance. The doctrine of forgiveness while turning the other cheek was considered a lot of nonsense; their mission in life was to scare the "hell" out of people, kindling terror and giving little children nightmares.

They did well at this. Their Holy Sabbath began at sundown on Saturday. Sunday worship was not just a midmorning service but an all-day session, with sermons lasting four or five hours as a prelude to marathon praying. And woe to anyone who fell asleep; he'd get a rap on the skull guaranteed to gift him with a bruised nob.

Part of a clergyman's responsibility was to preach strict obedience to the laws of the Bay Colony and to shock people with reminders of what terrible punishments lay in store for the lawbreakers. And in this area, the preachers had plenty to work with. The code of the Bay Colony led off with ten crimes punishable by death; these were murder, larceny, perjury, treason, bestiality, adultery, sodomy, blasphemy, witchcraft, and idolatry.

After working on this list of crimes for a few years, they added nine more that called for the death penalty: arson, repeated burglary, cursing or striking a parent, repeated denial of God, repeated highway robbery, return after exile (especially for Quakers and Jesuits), slave-stealing, rape of a maiden or an unmarried woman, and rebellion of a son against parental authority.

Meanwhile, at least until the early 1700s, there were various lesser crimes to be noted, along with such lesser punishments as the stocks, the ducking stool, the whipping post, burning, stoning, branding, crushing, disfiguring, and the breaking of bones. Christmas was outlawed. Santa Claus was exiled. Dancing, the drama, and merry music were banned. And a man was forbidden to kiss his wife in public or to kiss her even in private on Sundays, as a seafarer named Captain John Kemble discovered when he returned to Boston from a three-year voyage and greeted his wife with a hearty smack; he spent the rest of the day sitting in the stocks, charged with "lewd and unseemly behavior."

Certain of these laws and punishments had dropped into disuse by the 1700s, but even then, any hanging or other public execution was considered an occasion for everyone except the victim to turn out and relax and enjoy the spectacle. Some idea of the popularity of this spectator sport may be gleaned from the records of the distinguished Boston jurist Judge Samuel Sewall (who, incidentally, established a good foundation for his life's comfort by marrying the daughter of the town's mintmaster and receiving as dowry her weight in pine-tree shillings—$2,500). As Judge Sewall wrote in his diary in 1704:

"After dinner, about 3 p.m. I went to see the execution . . . . Many were the people that I saw upon Broughton's Hill. But when I came to see how the river was covered with people, I was amazed: Some say there were . . . . 150 boats and canoes . . . . When the scaffold was hoisted to a due height, the seven malefactors went up; Mr. Mather prayed for them standing upon the boat. Ropes were all fastened to the gallows . . . . When the scaffold was let to sink, there was such a screech of the women that my wife heard it sitting in our entry next the orchard. Our house is a full mile from the place."

Some screech.

Against all this background of violence, oppression, and religious fanaticism, the first dissenter to be injected into the history books with a push from colonial zealots was Roger Williams. He arrived in Boston in 1631 and promptly established himself as a troublemaking radical Separatist by refusing to join the Congregational Church. Instead, he hiked north to Salem to earn his living as an independent preacher and then sailed south to Plymouth, where he had second thoughts and decided to join the church after all.

By 1633, though, he was back in the pulpits of Salem again as independent as ever, and now he was arguing that the red cross in the English flag was a symbol of Antichrist and should be eliminated forthwith. This was a bit too much for the authorities to take; they ordered him into court on charges of having "divers dangerous opinions."

When Williams kept preaching in spite of this, the colonial authorities sent word to Salem commanding him to get down to Boston immediately and take ship back home to London.

"And sail across that ocean in midwinter?" said Williams. "Not me!"

He chose instead to slip off into the forest, depending upon his friends among the Indians to keep him reasonably warm and well fed until the weather improved. By the time the summer of 1636 rolled around, he was establishing himself as the first citizen of Providence, which he and his followers had founded. He stayed on to lead and govern for 45 years what was to become the colony of Rhode Island and Providence Plantations. (In 1936, the Massachusetts legislature voted to grant Williams a pardon and revoked the order of banishment passed 300 years before.)

Meanwhile, the Boston colonials had found another freethinker to get riled up about. This time their target was Anne Hutchinson, the Women's Lib leader of her day, who arrived in Boston in September 1634 and shortly made public her opinion that most preachers in the Bay Colony were chauvinist hypocrites. The mother of 14 children, Anne was a lady of good background who persisted in voicing her belief that salvation came from the individual's faith alone—contrary to the teachings of the Puritan Fathers. When she disliked a Sunday sermon, she'd walk out on it. Not only that, but she set up a series of weekly meetings in her home, at which she and other women of the Bay Colony would discuss the sermons of the previous Sunday, going so far as to analyze them for errors and hypocrisy.

To put down this show of independence, the Boston ministers gathered in conference one day and issued a regulation stating that "though women might meet (some few of them together) to pray and edify one another, yet such a set assembly (as was the practice at Boston) where 60 or more did meet every week and one woman (by resolving questions of doctrine and expounding Scripture) took upon her the whole exercise, was agreed to be disorderly and without rule."

This was their bureaucratic way of saying "Out, Anne! And don't come back!"

She was brought to trial and exiled. Refusing to deny her beliefs, she was also excommunicated from the church. After her husband's death, she settled on the shores of Pelham Bay, New York, with her younger children. There, she and her family, except for one daughter, were murdered by Mohawk Indians.

With such grim examples of bigotry and persecution on the books, it would seem that the intelligent thing for Quakers and Jesuits to have done would have been to stay as far away from Boston as possible. Instead, they seem to have headed for the Bay shore with all the crazy determination of a horse dashing back into a blazing stable.

The Quakers came first. Bay Colony history reports that they were "first noticed" in Massachusetts in 1656, "quaking and trembling at the word of God." And they were arrogantly following the precepts of their leading preacher, George Fox, the founder of the sect, who argued that "there is a light of Christ within each man's breast superior to bibles or sacraments"—and who prescribed that "Quakers shall not take off their hats in the presence of superiors. They should always use the familiar address (thee and thou) to all persons, no matter what their rank or position. They must not take an oath, even when required in court. They must not bend the knee, even to the King himself."

As if these rulings were not irritating enough to the authorities of Boston and Salem, the Quakers announced that their mission was "to save the superstitious Colony of Massachusetts with a message from the Lord—to fight against superstition and priestcraft."

But Massachusetts wasn't interested in being saved, at least not by Quakers. Instead of welcoming a chance for salvation, the Puritans were outraged. They viewed the Quakers as "pernicious heretics, with a gross collection of blasphemy and confusion."

Having voiced their opinions of the new arrivals, the Puritans put into operation a form of localized pogrom in which the Quakers were stripped of their clothes, robbed of their food, imprisoned, flogged, and ordered banished; and their books were "to be burned by the hangman in the market place." The captain of one ship that had brought them to the Bay Colony was seized and imprisoned and released only upon his solemn promise that he'd take them away again at his own expense. He didn't—because they wouldn't. Many chose instead to move along to Rhode Island, where they were reasonably certain of getting fair treatment at the hands of Roger Williams.

For those who remained in Massachusetts—and those exiles who might try to come back—the General Court in 1657 ruled that any man convicted of being a Quaker should have an ear cut off. Women were allowed to keep their ears but were sentenced to be stripped and whipped. A second conviction meant the loss of the other ear for the man and another stripping-whipping for the woman. If anyone, man or woman, were convicted a third time, the sentence called for piercing the tongue with a red-hot iron.

Despite all this, the jails were soon so overcrowded with convicted Quakers that the court decided to put them to work as a colonial labor force. Anyone refusing to work would get whipped twice a week thereafter—10 lashes the first time, 15 the second, 18 the third, and then in increments of three extra lashes each time around, until the victim gave in or just died.

The Quakers retaliated by prancing naked in the streets, smashing bottles in doorways, blackening their faces, and refusing to cut their hair to the length dictated by Puritan custom.

To this, the General Court in 1658 replied with an order that any banished Quaker who returned to the Bay Colony was to be executed. This was followed by a ruling that Quakers could be sold into slavery, to work the plantations of Virginia and the island of Barbados.

Within another few months, in 1659, two men and a woman who had been banished as Quakers returned to Massachusetts and were caught. The men were hanged and died singing as their necks broke; their clothes were hacked from their bodies with knives, and their corpses were thrown into an open pit on Boston Common and "left untended against the attacks of ravenous beasts." The woman was spared all this; she was merely stripped, whipped, and banished again.

The hangings went on and eventually included the killing of Mary Dyer, described in the records as "a comely, grave woman of good personage, who had braved death in Boston three times." Several others, who escaped the gallows, were stripped naked, tied to the tail of a cart, whipped through town, and sent on their way into the forest; those who returned and still persisted in trying to "save" Massachusetts were branded on the left shoulder.

After the founding of Pennsylvania as a Quaker refuge in 1681 and the passage in England of the Toleration Act in 1689, the persecution of Quakers declined and came virtually to an end, except for an occasional flogging. Religion of a more temperate form spread throughout Boston, until by 1750 the town had 17 church buildings and congregations, most of which utterly decried the other 16.

Meanwhile, the numbers of slaves and Jesuits were on the increase, providing fresh victims to take the place of the Quakers. In 1755, a black man and his wife were convicted of murdering their owner, Captain John Codman. The man was hanged, never realizing how lucky he was; the woman was burned alive. By 1765, there were 5,779 blacks in the Massachusetts Colony, almost all of whom were slaves, none of whom could walk abroad after nine o'clock at night, and any of whom could be trapped and shot like an animal if he tried to run away.

The Jesuits, for their part, were greatly feared and almost insanely abhorred. As late as 1770, the law held that any person associated with the church of Rome should stay out of the colony or risk life imprisonment; and if he escaped from prison, he was to be executed. The standard fine for any person caught giving shelter to a priest was the equivalent of $1,000.

This persecution of the Roman Catholic clergy gave rise to a popular Boston festival known as Pope Day, sort of an American substitution for England's Guy Fawkes Day. On Pope Day, effigies of the pope and the devil, marked for hanging and burning, were mounted on a platform and paraded through Boston's streets to the sounds of exploding firecrackers, cannon shots, and the howling and roistering of the mob.

This festival soon became so popular that it duplicated itself; instead of one parade, there were two, with cheering crowds stepping off simultaneously from the town's North End and South End. Inevitably they would collide somewhere near the center of town. Then would follow a battle royal, a melee of swinging clubs and fists, of flying bricks and bottles, of curses and screams, of broken jaws and bleeding heads. If the North End contingent won the fight, all the survivors would flock to Copp's Hill near the Old North Church for a sociable and peaceful end to the affair. If the South End won, everybody swarmed to Boston Common.

In either case, the celebration always came to an end with a great bonfire in which the effigies were burned. And the odor of brimstone lay heavy on the town.

It's not surprising that at least one street corner has retained the distinction of that label.

Grave Sites and Grave Slights

A CEMETERY is supposed to be a place of solitude and rest. But during almost any summer day, up to 5,000 persons who are walking the Freedom Trail will turn left through the iron-arch entrance of Boston's Granary Burying Ground and start wandering among centuries-old gravestones and burial plots.

What brings them there is the chance to visit the graves of figures known to them only through history books and childhood impressions.

What brought the dead people there is the fact that there was no room for them in the Bay Colony's first burial ground, diagonally across the street at King's Chapel.

That Chapel cemetery was originally the vegetable garden of one of the first Boston settlers, Sir Isaac Johnson, who built his house in 1630 on land presently occupied by Boston's Old City Hall. He died within the year, and his friends, obeying his deathbed wish, planted him where he had earlier planted his corn and pumpkins.

Sir Isaac must have been extremely popular, for as soon as they had buried him, his friends decided they'd like to be buried beside him. They pointed out that Isaac's garden was pretty much of a failure anyhow. "Brother Johnson's garden is getting to be a poor place for vegetables," they wrote. So why not put the land to more practical use? Nobody offered any objections, and thus was created Boston's first official cemetery.

By 1660, so many people had been put to rest in Johnson's potato patch that there was no longer room for any more graves. The Town Fathers thereupon turned their eyes to a spot just a short distance southwest of Johnson's land on a section of Boston Common that was being used for the storing of grain. It was a simple matter to shovel some of the grain aside and to designate the cleared area as the town's new cemetery.

And so there came into being a burial ground that is not only one of the oldest in the original colonies but also one of the most unusual in terms of occupants whose names were directly associated with colonial history and the fight for freedom.

Here are buried such people as Josiah Franklin and his wife, the parents of Benjamin Franklin; James Otis, whose fiery speeches against the Crown and the Writs of Assistance in 1761 were the opening sounds of the Revolution; Peter Faneuil and Paul Revere; three signers of the Declaration of Independence, namely John Hancock, Sam Adams, and Robert Treat Paine; Crispus Attucks, the first casualty of the Boston Massacre, as well as its other victims; early governors and jurists; and, of all people, "Mother Goose."

The name on the Mother Goose gravestone is a simple Mary Goose. Despite documented research to the contrary, most people prefer to believe that this woman, the wife of Isaac Vergoose, was the little old lady whose nursery rhymes have been delighting children for years. Tradition says that these rhymes were first published in Boston by the printer Thomas Fleet in 1719.

Of the thousands of visitors who move along the Freedom Trail each week and who pause to examine the historical gravestones in Old Granary, more ask to be shown the grave of Mother Goose than ask for that of any other individual.

Old Granary is always a corner of calm and peace. It is an ideal place to pause and rest, to enjoy the sheltering shadows of the Park Street Church on one hand and the Boston Athenaeum library on the other, to experience some of the quiet feeling of being in a country churchyard, to listen to the singing of birds and the music of steeple chimes, and to ignore the noisy confusion of street traffic just beyond the gate. Panhandlers, winos, and loud-tongued shoppers seldom intrude.

But if the Granary Burying Ground has been nurtured on peace and quiet, precisely the opposite is true of the Freedom Trail site diagonally across the way, King's Chapel. This church, standing where Sir Isaac Johnson once raised cabbages and cucumbers, was born and thrived on a diet of storm, strife, and dissension.

It must have been a beautiful chapel when it was first built. It was constructed of golden-brown granite, and it is still beautiful, even though its granite blocks some years ago turned a gloomy gray under the darkening of age, weather, and city smoke.

The Chapel had its beginning back in the 1680s, when King James II achieved the ultimate in royal stupidity by sending to Boston a chaplain whose mission was to establish in the town the very thing the Puritans had hated and fled—the Church of England.

The roar of protest was so loud and furious that it's a wonder the king himself didn't hear it. But it would have made no difference to him if he had; he'd decided there was going to be a Church of England Meeting House in Boston even if he had to construct it of Puritan bones.

While the unwelcome chaplain, the Reverend Robert Ratcliffe, was trying to unpack his trunks with one hand and ward off dissenters with the other, over from London came a new royal governor, Sir Edmund Andros. The Puritans probably would have preferred Beelzebub.

"Where do you plan to build the meeting house?" Andros asked Ratcliffe in effect.

"It can't be done, m'Lord," said Ratcliffe. "These crazy colonials won't cede or sell us an inch of their land."

"Who cares?" said Andros. "If they won't let us build a church, we'll take the one they're using."

And Andros did. He led his guards to the Old South Meeting House, took the keys from the sexton by force, and announced that the place thereafter would be used for the Episcopalian services of the Church of England—and if any misguided Puritans wanted to conduct their Congregationalist services there on Sundays, they could bloody well wait outside until the Anglicans were through.

This awkward situation lasted for two years; the Episcopalians held forth in Old South, while the Puritans stood outside muttering imprecations for five or six hours each Sunday, waiting for an end to the interlopers' marathon preaching and praying.

Meanwhile, Andros, deciding he liked the look of Sir Isaac Johnson's sloping farmland as a possible site for a new church, proceeded in 1688 to grab by right of eminent domain that portion of the vegetable garden that was not yet being used for burial plots. And that's where the original wooden King's Chapel was completed in 1689.

According to the records, the structure was quite dilapidated by 1741. This prompted the town's wealthiest merchant, Peter Faneuil, to start a subscription fund for the construction of a new church to be built of stone. Architect Peter Harrison of Newport, Rhode Island, was commissioned to design the structure.

The whole building procedure, from raising the money to getting the stones in place, was a slow process. The huge, four-foot-thick granite blocks, quarried in Quincy eight miles to the south, were shipped by barge to Boston, which was quite an engineering feat in itself and caused the people of Quincy to scream that they were being robbed of their precious stone and that it would all go to the bottom of the sea. But it didn't. The blocks were off-loaded at the Boston waterfront and hauled uphill by teams of eight oxen. The cornerstone finally was laid on August 1, 1749, to the accompaniment of loud jeers and much hurling of cow manure on the part of the Puritan spectators.

The granite church was then built around and over the original wooden structure, and when all the stone blocks were in place the wooden church inside was torn down and thrown out of the windows.

In 1754, the granite King's Chapel was officially opened in a setting of military braid, scarlet uniforms, beautiful gowns, and an abundance of plaques bearing British coats of arms. Again the Puritans were on hand to throw garbage and dead animals at the doors and windows.

From the very start, it had become something of a hobby for British royalty to lavish gifts upon King's Chapel. King James II had presented a costly pulpit. William and Mary had given the church 100 pounds a year outright and sent gifts of communion silver, altar cloths, carpets, and cushions. Queen Anne came through with expensive red cushions and vestments. King George III in time added more silver communion pieces.

Many of the costly and irreplaceable items owned by King's Chapel in its early years are still in use today, including a magnificent communion table that was carved out of oak and built in 1686. Pews that were occupied on the original day of dedication are still in use, with benches that face toward each other to provide their occupants a chance to ease their cold feet in wintertime by sharing charcoal foot warmers.

In 1713, Thomas Brattle, treasurer of Harvard College, gave the church its first organ. Unfortunately, there were no organists in Massachusetts, and King's Chapel had to send to England to request "a sober person that can play skillfully with a loud noise." Meanwhile, the organ stood in the Chapel vestibule for seven months. People didn't like it there. They said it was "a box of whistles, and the devil is in it."

The Chapel's original silver disappeared in the early days of Revolutionary troubles, along with the Reverend Henry Caner, who had taken over as minister in 1747. The Reverend Caner was an outspoken Loyalist sympathizer. As such, he was informed by a delegation of Patriots one morning that he had exactly seven hours to pack up and leave the church in which he had served for almost 30 years. He hastily took off for Halifax, taking with him 30 of the Tory families among his parishioners and all of the King's Chapel records and silver. The records were recovered years later in London, but no trace was ever found of the precious communion silver. If anybody knows where it is, the Chapel would like to get it back.

After the good Reverend Caner had departed with the silver, King's Chapel was left with no ordained minister to hold things together. This situation dragged on for two years, until the churchgoers at last held an emergency meeting and appointed their senior warden, Dr. Thomas Bulfinch, father of the State House architect, to find someone to fill the pulpit. Bulfinch decided upon James Freeman, a brilliant lay preacher from Salem who was attending Harvard Divinity School.

Freeman accepted the job and brought with him to Boston some rather radical ideas about theology. One of these was his contention that the English Book of Common Prayer, in standard use by Episcopalians, contained several gross errors, the gravest of which was the dogma of the Trinity.

Freeman proceeded to rewrite the prayer book with a version of his own, knocking out the Trinity along with all references to special prayers for the king and queen.

King's Chapel thereupon stopped being Trinitarian and became Unitarian, the first such church in America. However, it was to be another 40 years before the Unitarian denomination would come into being as a formal body.

The uproar over Freeman's revision of the prayer book was so clamorous that in 1787 the Episcopalian hierarchy denounced him and his followers as heretics, cut the Chapel loose from the Church of England, and of course flatly refused to ordain the young preacher. King's Chapel parishioners shrugged, and ordained Freeman themselves.

In the midst of all this confusion, the Roman Catholic church achieved an unexpected entry into the Chapel records. That happened in September 1778 when a funeral Mass was celebrated for Chevalier de St. Sauveur, a French naval adjutant and chamberlain to Count d'Artois, brother of the King of France.

St. Sauveur, serving aboard the French frigate *La Nymphe,* was killed on September 8 in a Boston street riot when he and a group of sailors sought to obtain supplies of bread for the French ships in the harbor. Bostonians, who hated the Catholic religion and distrusted the presence of French warships in port, clubbed the young nobleman to death.

The Massachusetts House of Representatives, fearing an international incident, immediately voted to erect a monument in honor of St. Sauveur and even seemed favorably inclined toward holding a public Mass in his memory. The idea of the Mass was quickly rejected by the French admiral Count d'Estaing, who reasoned there was enough trouble going on already without asking for more.

To close the case as quickly as possible, a funeral Mass was held in secret at ten o'clock on the night of September 15, and St. Sauveur was laid to rest in a King's Chapel crypt known as the "Stranger's Vault." A Franciscan priest was the celebrant. The Mass was the first ever held in a Boston church.

The secretary of the French fleet wrote of the occasion:

"Eight sailors of the *'Tonnant'* bore the coffin on their shoulders preceded by the sexton and the grave digger. The servant of the deceased followed. We started in that order at 10 o'clock and arriving at King's Chapel found the basement illuminated with many candles.

"The vault was opened and the reverend father deposited the remains without ceremony. The door of the vault having been closed and padlocked, we returned to sign the register of interment which had been drawn up."

St. Sauveur didn't lack for company in his crypt; 30 other skeletons were found there some years ago when the tomb was opened for repairs. Nobody knows who they were or why they were so entombed.

As for the St. Sauveur monument, the Massachusetts legislature finally got around to erecting it at King's Chapel 139 years later, after the French government had asked where it was—they wanted to send flowers.

The St. Sauveur monument, incidentally, is crowned with a steeplelike obelisk, which is more than can be said for the Chapel itself. A design for a steeple was included in architect Harrison's original plans, but somehow it never got built, even though George Washington himself contributed five pounds toward getting the job done right. Somebody got the money, but the Chapel got no steeple.

Another oddity of the Chapel is the dark, cramped, airless little cell that has been walled over by a black marble slab at the rear of the church. Criminals who had been sentenced to death used to be brought there in chains on the Sunday before their execution and made to sit inside and listen to the lengthy sermon of the day, which usually dwelt upon the rottenness of the guilty man's character and the fitness of his reward. Then the doomed wretch would be paraded to Boston Common to be hanged.

Thus from Sir Isaac Johnson's worthless potato patch has emerged one of Boston's most interesting historic sites. The original vegetable garden still holds the remains of many well-known Boston figures—Governor John Winthrop, first head of the Bay Colony; Lady Andros, wife of the hated royal governor; William

Dawes, Jr., who finished the ride that Paul Revere began; Robert Keayne, first commander of the Ancient and Honorable Artillery Company; Mary Chilton, traditionally the first woman to step on Plymouth Rock; the Puritan minister John Cotton; several relatives of Paul Revere; and many others.

But it's a waste of time to try to find their graves. In 1934, as part of Franklin D. Roosevelt's WPA program, a gang of workmen arrived at the Chapel burial ground one morning to clean up the premises and put things in order.

They did. They dug up all the gravestones and replanted them in precise orderly rows. Now nobody knows where any of the bodies are buried, including that of Sir Isaac himself—who probably never would have spaded up his first potato if he'd known what a busy place his vegetable garden was going to become.

From Cave to Culture

THE MOST DISTINCTIVE DIFFERENCE between the Pilgrims who landed at Plymouth in 1620 and the Puritans who founded Boston in 1630 lay in their socio-economic backgrounds. The Puritans, as a group, came from comfortable English families and were reasonably well educated. The Pilgrims, on the other hand, were dirt poor and generally unschooled. Thus the first thing on the schedule for Plymouth Colony was for everybody to get to work and produce food. But one of the first things undertaken by the settlers of the Massachusetts Bay Colony was to consider their children's future. And that meant putting the youngsters into school as quickly as possible.

When it came to selecting a site for a schoolhouse, the Town Fathers of Boston did what a number of other land-grabbers were to do in years to come; they took a look at the sunny slope of Sir Isaac Johnson's farmland and exclaimed, "Just what we need!" So saying, they founded the Boston Public Latin School in 1635 and erected America's first public schoolhouse just a few yards east of King's Chapel Burying Ground. The following year the Massachusetts legislature proceeded to vote the funds necessary to establish a college. Thus was Harvard University born, receiving its name through the death of the Reverend John Harvard in September 1638 and his bequest to the college of his 400-volume library and half of his estate, some 800 pounds.

The popular conception is that Harvard—it became a university in 1780—and the other early New England colleges were established primarily to train ministers for the colonial churches and to provide a steady supply of clergymen independent of England. While this is true in part, there were cultural and economic aims that went far beyond this premise. The New England colleges did train ministers and kept a good supply moving out to the towns and villages, but the schools were not theological seminaries as such.

For example, the General Court Charter of 1650, which incorporated Harvard, did not specify that its purpose was to train students for the ministry. There were other needs as well, and these included trained teachers, jurists, writers, doctors, and other professionals. In general, the objectives were to advance learning and to pass it along to posterity. The Charter of 1650 speaks of the need to educate both English and Indian youths in knowledge as well as godliness and to advance the arts and sciences. Ministers would emerge from this program, true. But the fact is that less than half of all the 17th-century alumni of Harvard entered the pulpit.

Meanwhile, students entering Harvard faced a curriculum that would terrify the average college student today. Among the required subjects were grammar, logic, rhetoric, religion, arithmetic, geometry, astronomy, metaphysics, ethics, natural science, Greek, Hebrew, and ancient history. In those days, nobody studied Latin at Harvard. A student was expected to learn that language in grammar school and to speak it freely in his Harvard classroom. And if he got mixed up in his gerunds or gerundives or ablative absolutes, he could expect a caning that would raise blisters.

Despite this grim prospect, students struggled hard to get into college and to stay there. The tuition at Harvard in 1655 was two pounds. Lacking cash, a student could come up with the equivalent in terms of wheat, beef, furs, firewood, turnips, goats, apples, butter, rum, or whatnot.

This early concern with education conforms to the Puritans' determination that their children, growing up in the colonies, should enjoy the freedom and the opportunity to advance themselves to whatever social and economic benefits lay within reach of their talents. It was the utter antithesis of the European system, which held that a youngster should be content to live his life on the level to which he was born and not get any impudent ideas about self-improvement.

That traditional European attitude was one of the prime reasons why the Puritans had left England in the first place—to stake out a better life in the freedom of the colonies.

In the early years, there must have been many times when that "better life" seemed hopelessly beyond reach. Most of the Boston settlers had good family backgrounds in England, families that had produced educators, clergymen, lawyers, doctors, writers, jurists. But regardless of breeding or background, those who were the first to arrive on the shores of Boston Bay didn't have even a lean-to in which to live. They were homeless in a strange land, without a place to sleep.

For immediate shelter, they had no choice then but to dig a hole in the ground or a cave in a hillside. They would roof this and wall it, leaving a doorway space to be covered by animal skins or spare sail canvas or whatever else might be handy.

With this for a start, they would gradually add corner posts and above-ground siding, cut holes for windows covered over with oiled paper, build a fireplace (with a wooden chimney!), chink up all the drafty openings with mud, and in time rebuild the whole miserable structure with hand-hewn planks, glacial stones, and a thatched roof. Out of all this, eventually, there somehow came the graceful design known today as colonial architecture—plus various individual houses which were built so solidly that they're still in use after almost three centuries of blizzards, hurricanes, heat, ice, salt fog, and riots.

Life was stark and crude in those early homes. Everything centered around the huge fireplace, which was kept burning night and day all through the year, both for cooking and for midwinter heating. Floors, which were usually packed dirt, were damp and cold and unsanitary—although nice children were always brought up to "spit in the corner." What feeble light existed after sundown came from fireplace flames, blazing pine knots, and homemade tallow candles that were absolutely unbeatable at producing greasy smoke.

At the dining table, cutlery and dishes were scarce; a quick hand was what counted. A bowl of venison stew might be placed in the center of the table, at which point everybody would dive in with fingers and hunting knives, trusting that nobody would lose a thumb in the excitement. Parents and adult guests always sat above the salt and did all the talking; children and servants sat below the salt, under strict orders to eat quickly in silence and to leave the room as soon as possible. Rum, wine, or beer might be passed around the table, with everybody drinking in turn from the same bowl.

By 1650, barely two decades after this primitive start, the record showed gains that were almost beyond belief. During this short span of time, the settlers had worked so hard and so fruitfully that gracious homes had been built and tastefully furnished, schools were in operation throughout the area, steepled churches were thriving, iron was being forged, blown glass was available, servants and slaves had been imported, books were being printed, housewives were demanding stylish gowns of silks and satin, and— thanks to a remarkable welfare system—literally nobody was a pauper. Meanwhile, some 50,000 people had come from England to live beside the shores of the bay.

The welfare system in the Bay Colony was a unique creation of the Puritans themselves, not borrowed from any other society. And it worked.

It was based on the principle that everybody must be cared for—that a person down on his luck should not be treated as a criminal or a born loser but should be given a helping hand by his neighbors, no matter where he happened to live or how big were his troubles. The law specified that no orphan should go homeless or unschooled. No man who was able to work went jobless. No widow went hungry. The Bay Colony welfare system took care of everybody. A poverty class simply did not exist.

Naturally, as in any society, the passing of years and the changing of circumstances produced individual cases that, if not taken care of, would have threatened the Colony with a serious pauper problem. Men died and left widows, parents died and left orphans, old age and sickness left proud men unable to work, shiftless immigrants arrived from England.

But the Colony passed laws to keep this situation under control. There was so much work to be done, in the fields and in the woods and in the homes as well, that the problem of filling jobs was much greater than the problem of finding them. The work laws took this into consideration. If a man flatly refused to do any work, he faced the choice of sitting in the stocks and getting pelted with garbage or of slipping out of town before he could get caught. If an orphan lacked a home of his own, there was always another home just down the road where his labor would be welcomed in exchange for food, housing, and an education. If a widow had no place to turn, she would be assigned as a domestic in some busy home or she could expect to be auctioned off to any family willing to support her in exchange for labor. In view of the alternatives, few people tried to get by on handouts. There was plenty of work for everybody.

Inevitably, however, families acquiring wealth and success began to emerge and to move ahead of their middle-class neighbors. Men who could offer employment became the leaders and bosses of men who needed to be employed. And the wives of the more successful townsmen began wearing much better finery than the gray dresses and white caps worn by the women in the less successful Puritan families. To keep up with their wives, the men of wealth and influence began to sport all kinds of accessories and ornamental trimmings, from gold lace to silver-buckled shoes and from silk-lined jackets to flowing hair styles.

As early as 1634, this sort of thing was already getting so far out of hand that the General Court passed special laws ordering men and women alike to cut down on their ostentatious apparel and their decorative growths of hair.

The Puritan clergy were quick to applaud this action by the lawmakers and to ridicule those colonists who were trying to outdo the fashion plates of London and Paris. One outspoken minister, Nathaniel Ward of Agawam, felt compelled to editorialize for the records:

"When I hear a nugatory gentle-dame inquire what dress the Queen is in this week, what the fashion of the Court—I mean the very newest—with eagerness to be in it with all haste, whatever it may be, I look at her as the very gizzard of a trifle, the product of a quarter of a cypher, the epitome of nothing, fitter to be kicked (if she were of a kickable nature) than either honored or humored.

"It is beyond my understanding to conceive how those women should have any true grace, or valuable virtue, that have so little wit as to disfigure themselves with such exotic garb as not only dismantles their native lovely luster but transclouts them into gaunt bar-geese, ill-shapen shellfish, Egyptian hieroglyphs, or at best French flirts, which a proper English woman should scorn with her heels.

"I can make myself sick at any time by comparing the dazzling splendor wherewith our gentlewomen were embellished in former habits with the gut-foundered goosedom wherewith they are now surcingled and debauched. We have many of them in our Colony. If I see any of them accidentally, I cannot cleanse my fancy of them for a month after.

"I have been a solitary widower for almost twelve years, intending lately to make a trip back to my native country; but when I consider how women have tripe-wifed themselves with their cladments, I have no heart for the voyage, lest their nauseous shapes and the sea should work too sorely upon my stomach. I speak sadly."

The fashion fanatics, having been roundly rebuked both by the General Court and the general clergy, bowed humbly to the scoldings; and for a short time thereafter, they trudged around in the same kind of subdued clothing that everybody else was wearing. But this phase did not last. Well before the mid-1600s were over, the increase in the power and number of certain wealthy families had provided them with the freedom to ignore the laws and to institute new peacocky fads. Buckles, baubles, and ruffs returned to stay.

Meanwhile, with the establishing of the Boston Public Latin School and with the passing of strict laws requiring a grammar school for every community of 50 families, the colonists had planted the seed from which Boston culture was to grow and flourish with astonishing speed.

In 1638, the Colony's first printing press was set up in Cambridge. In 1674, the General Court authorized a printing press for Boston. By the end of the 1600s, more than 300 publications had been printed; bookstores in Boston were selling Boston-printed products and also importing a tremendous variety of volumes from abroad.

Meanwhile, the Latin School was sending many of its graduates across the Charles River to continue their studies at Harvard, just as it does today more than 300 years later. And among its students in the pre-Revolution years were such future freedom-seekers as Sam Adams, John Hancock, and Benjamin Franklin, whose prolific parents lived just a short walk from the Latin School, down the hillside and toward the waterfront. A plaque on the Freedom Trail marks the site of the house where Franklin was born in 1706, the 15th offspring in his parents' production line of 17 children.

Franklin didn't stay around Boston very long. In addition to flying kites and helping his father manufacture soap, Benjamin at the age of 16 was also writing articles for the *New England Courant,* a Boston newspaper being printed by his brother James. James, however, didn't think very highly of his young brother's literary ability and so rejected most of his writings. To overcome this handicap, Ben adopted the pen name of Silence Dogood and used to hustle to his brother's printshop before dawn to slide the Dogood pieces under the door for James to discover in the morning. James thought these articles were great, certainly far better than anything young Ben could write. And Silence Dogood became a regular feature in the *Courant.*

After putting up with this nonsense for a year or so, Benjamin quit his job as apprentice to James and took off in disgust to try his luck in New York but ended up in Philadelphia. Boston has had to settle for the plaque marking his birthplace and for the portrait statue, also on the Freedom Trail, by Richard S. Greenough that stands on the lawn of the Old City Hall, on the left of the Trail pathway.

That Old City Hall, incidentally, is no longer in use; a new, modern-design structure has been erected in nearby Government Center. But some of the classic political stories that used to emanate from the Old City Hall may never be replaced, especially those concerning Boston's most flamboyant politician of recent times and the city's oft-recurring mayor, the late James Michael

Curley. A word about him (and a typical story) before passing
Old City Hall . . . . .

Curley was one of Boston's most fervent all-time champions
of freedom of speech and free thought, particularly when the
speech and the thoughts were his own. This philosophy not only
placed him in the mayor's office from time to time but also put
him in the Massachusetts governor's chair and in a congressional
seat as well. The fact that *his* ideas of freedom occasionally brought
him a political setback and once even landed him in the federal
prison at Danbury—for mail fraud—didn't change his philosophy
a bit. He always said what he felt like saying.

Curley also had a remarkable talent for bringing other men's
careers to an abrupt halt with just a few well-timed words. One
of his better performances in this respect dealt with a City Hall
hanger-on and political lackey named Lafferty, who for several
years back in the 1940s had been living well on the odd jobs
that were tossed his way by the Curley political machine and on
handouts from favor seekers who seemed to think that Lafferty
had a direct line to Curley's ear.

On this occasion, with another mayoral election about to come up,
the anti-Curley reformists were whipping together big strength
throughout Boston, and it appeared that James Michael was
going to be handed one of his occasional defeats, perhaps the
worst of his career.

The closer the clock moved toward Election Day, the gloomier
the situation looked for Curley. Lafferty watched what was happen-
ing, weighed the possibilities, and finally decided that Curley was
going to get trounced so badly he'd never return to power again.
So Lafferty, figuring it was a case of every man for himself, de-
serted the City Hall machine that had employed him and threw
all of his energies into the support of the reformist candidate.

The election that year was close, but Curley won. And Lafferty,
aghast at the mistake he had made, immediately hurried to City
Hall to plead for Curley's forgiveness.

At first, Curley refused to see him. He kept Lafferty sitting in
a waiting room for better than a week, scorned by all the City
Hall regulars and looking more penitent and discouraged every
day.

Finally, one morning, Curley called newsmen to his office and sent for Lafferty, who sidled in with his head bowed and immediately began to babble about how sorry he was.

"Shut up," Curley told him curtly. Then he turned to the newsmen. "I know all of you boys are familiar with the Lafferty situation," he said in his Oxonian accent, "and I suppose some of you have been wondering what I would do about it. After all, Lafferty and I were friends for years. He did me many favors, and I did him many favors. Such things are hard to forget. Old friends should take care of each other."

"God bless the man!" Lafferty cried.

"Well," said Curley, ignoring him, "I've called you reporters here today because I want you to know I've found just the right spot for my friend Mr. Lafferty. I'm going to see that he gets something useful to do and in a prominent position where his true abilities will be noticed."

"The soul of forgiveness!" Lafferty murmured. "What a kind man indeed!"

"Shut up," said Curley. "Shut up and listen to me. As I was walking to work through our fair city this glorious morning, I was thinking about your case, Lafferty, and I was wondering just where you'd fit in. And then, Lafferty old friend, suddenly I had the answer. It came to me as I was strolling past the Jordan Marsh department store on Washington Street. I tell you, Lafferty, it was like an inspiration.

"You see, Lafferty, I noticed that they were dressing a big show window at Jordan Marsh. And you know what?—They need another headless dummy!"

Such was life at the Old City Hall, teaching lessons that were never in the Latin School curriculum.

Downhill from the original site of the Latin School is a beautifully preserved colonial structure that became famous more than a century ago as the Old Corner Book Store.

This ancient brick building occupies land that once belonged to Anne Hutchinson. She lived there from 1634 to the sad day in 1638 when she left town en route to her death appointment with the Mohawk Indians.

The home which she was forced to leave was burned to the ground in a big fire that struck Boston on October 3, 1711. While the ruins were still warm, the land was bought by a wealthy pharmacist and real-estate opportunist named Dr. Thomas Crease, who built the present structure about 1712 as a combination residence and apothecary shop.

Dr. Crease lived in the back of the house and parceled out his pills and potions in the front room. Presumably he stocked all of the customary weird medicines of that period—live leeches, crude opium, and the entire run of herbs from mandrake to chamomile—and used them in concocting his remedies. He died a rich man; how his patients may have died is not recorded.

The building subsequently had several owners, one of whom used it for a dry-goods store, another who turned it back into a residence, and still another who changed it back into an apothecary shop again.

In 1828, the building finally began to move toward its special destiny, for it was in that year that the structure was leased to a firm of booksellers known as Carter & Handee. Five years later it was acquired by a book publisher named William Ticknor, who made a fortune by taking in as partner another publisher, James T. Fields, and launching upon the American literary market such authors as Hawthorne, Lowell, Longfellow, Dickens, and Thackeray.

Fields was a brilliant man, a remarkable author himself and a learned conversationalist. He set aside a ground-floor office, defined only by green curtains; and from that spot, he began editing a magazine called the *Atlantic Monthly*, turning out the new publication on presses that were driven literally by horse power—a team of two Canadian horses, liberally stoked with oats and hay.

Under Ticknor and Fields, the bookstore soon became the favorite meeting place for all the great writers of New England and for all the great writers from other places who might be passing through Boston. Visitors to the store, through the years of its fame and popularity, might have expected at various times to find Emerson there or Trollope or Whittier, Stowe, Alcott, Agassiz, or any other distinguished author of the times.

Today, with its brick exterior tastefully and accurately restored, the Old Corner Book Store stands not only as a direct link with Boston's colonial origin but also as a revered wellspring of the Golden Age of American Literature.

Back in 1960, the structure was almost destroyed; incredibly, the plans for Boston's massive downtown redevelopment program called for Old Corner to be torn down and to be replaced either by a high-rise motel or a new federal office building.

Upon learning of this, Bostonians rose up with a roaring "No!" Almost overnight, they raised the money to save Old Corner from demolition and to preserve it as a permanent part of the Freedom Trail and the rich heritage of Boston culture.

The people of Boston can be very stubborn about things like that. When they feel they're being pushed around, they seize upon the right and freedom to shove back.

Old South and Its Mouth

NO ONE WHO EVER HEARD Calvin Coolidge make a speech would have called the President an exciting orator. He was strictly a reader and a dull one at that. He proved this every time he addressed a public audience.

One such occasion was a speech he made shortly after sundown on May 11, 1919, at the closing ceremonies of the 250th anniversary celebration of Boston's Old South Church. Coolidge was Governor of Massachusetts at the time, quite unaware that he would soon be propelled into national prominence by his quelling of the Boston police strike and his sharp telegram to labor leader Samuel Gompers, which read: *"There is no right to strike against the public safety by anybody, anywhere, any time."*

Coolidge was somewhat less than sharp, though, on that May night at the contemporary Old South Church in Boston's Back Bay area with his drab reference to its parent body and its original place of worship, the Old South Meeting House.

"You had a historical location there on Washington Street near the Old State House," he reminded his listeners. "Revolutionary leaders including Samuel Adams met under its roof and spoke for liberty. All great causes which this church has approved have always been successful in the end. It has a great history and has formed a great part in the making of the nation. It is indeed a grateful task to come here and bring the greetings of the Commonwealth of Massachusetts."

Dry stuff indeed, though wholly accurate; and appropriately enough, it was being delivered by a man whose paternal ancestors had been among the first English settlers to arrive in the Bay Colony in 1630.

Those ancestors of Coolidge, however, would have attended services at Old South Meeting House, which was the heart and center of colonial Congregationalism long before Old South Church was built. It was a place where freedom acquired strong, outspoken champions and where the British acquired headaches and earaches.

The original Meeting House was the first of three homes to be used by the Old South parish. It was a small structure, built of hand-cut cedar boards and erected on land where the Freedom Trail now passes the intersection of Washington and Milk streets, just a few steps from the birthplace of many little Franklins, including the one named Benjamin.

The site originally was part of a sloping cornfield and potato patch owned and tilled by the Bay Colony's first Governor, John Winthrop. Upon his death in March 1649, the land passed into the hands of a fluid-tongued preacher named John Norton, who was once described by the Reverend Cotton Mather as "the chief of our burning and shining lights."

Preacher Norton's light went out in April 1663. The land then became the property of his widow, Mary, who generously donated it to the original Old South parishioners when they were looking around for a place on which to build their first Meeting House. No doubt if she hadn't offered the property as a site, the parishioners would have settled their land-search problem in the fashion of the day by hiking up the hill and staking out a claim on Sir Isaac Johnson's vegetable garden.

For the first eight years of its existence, Old South was led by a minister named Thomas Thatcher, who was also a physician. His ability to mend bodies as well as spirits was further enhanced by his persuasive skill as a preacher, "gifted especially in prayer," the old records recall.

Thatcher was succeeded in 1678 by Samuel Willard, who left his mark upon the church so indelibly that even today he is still referred to in terms of highest respect. In fact, on that May night in 1919 when Coolidge was boring an Old South audience with his dull address, the then pastor of the church, Dr. George A. Gordon, described Willard as "altogether the greatest minister of the church throughout the colonial period."

Willard, who had graduated from Harvard at the age of 18, was to serve Old South for more than 29 years, until his death in 1707. Toward the end of his life, he was offered the presidency of Harvard; but rather than leave his Old South parish and move across the river to Cambridge, he turned the offer down.

There were many dramatic and colorful moments in the ministerial life of Willard and in that of the Old South parishioners in his flock.

One of those incidents took place in 1696, when Judge Samuel Sewall stood up in his pew box on a Sunday morning and listened to a public reading of his confession of guilt and remorse for having presided over a Salem witchcraft trial.

Actually, Judge Sewall's role as a persecutor of witches had been quite minor; he had conducted one trial only and then had withdrawn, sickened by the whole business. But his participation had taken place during the black year of 1692, when 13 women and 6 men had been convicted of witchcraft and hanged; one man was pressed to death beneath glacial boulders. Judge Sewall's association with the hysteria of that time was a burden to him for four years, until the day of his public and contrite apology, as read by Samuel Willard at an Old South prayer meeting:

"Samuel Sewall, sensible of the reiterated strokes of God upon himself and family, and being sensible that as to the guilt contracted upon the opening of the late Court of Oyer and Terminer ["emergency" witch-court] at Salem he is upon many accounts more concerned than any he knows of, desires to take the blame and shame of it. Asking pardon of men, and especially desiring prayers that God, who has an unlimited authority, would pardon that sin and all of his other sins, personal and relative. And according to His infinite benignity and sovereignty, not visit the sin of him, or of any other, upon himself or any of his, nor upon the land. But that He would powerfully defend him against all temptations to sin for the future; and vouchsafe him the efficacious, saving conduct of His word and spirit."

At the conclusion of the reading, Judge Sewall acknowledged the words with a deep submissive bow.

Another event of historic significance occurred on a bitterly cold, blizzardy, midwinter morning when Willard baptized a squawling baby named Benjamin Franklin. As Dr. Gordon described it: "This little quivering mass of flesh, hardly a day old, was carried across the wintry street to be baptized on the 6th of January, 1706, the parents evidently thinking that the mid-winter climate here was less to be dreaded than the climate in the other world."

Still another high spot in Willard's leadership came when he and his followers finally rebelled at the tyrannical tactics of Governor Edmund Andros. Fed up with his taking over their little church and giving the Episcopalians priority in its use, they physically prodded Andros aboard a ship in Boston Harbor and sent him packing home to England as an undesirable citizen—which he certainly was.

Willard was famed too for his generosity in taking up special Sunday collections for the widows and children of seagoing parishioners who had been killed in battles with pirates. If a first collection fell short of his expectations, he'd order a second. This form of colonial "social security" was quite effective in converting nonbelievers into devout Congregationalists.

After 60 years of service, the old cedar-board Meeting House was pulled down in March 1729, and work was begun on a new structure, to be built of brick and fashioned after the style of the graceful English churches designed by Sir Christopher Wren.

Thus a "new" Old South was dedicated on April 26, 1730, destined for a place in American annals not only as a historic church but also as probably the most important Meeting House in American colonial history. It was a tasteful place of worship, and it was also big enough to handle political meetings that drew crowds in the thousands.

Straightway, Old South became a place for clamorous gatherings of the colonists whenever they became overangry, overoutraged, or overfrightened.

One such assembly was hurriedly called to order by the Reverend Thomas Prince in October 1746 when word reached Boston that a French fleet was bearing down on the port, apparently intent on invasion.

Having neither the time nor the weapons to mount an effective defense, the colonists gambled their fate on Prince's ability to pray up a storm that would wreck the fleet. Parson Prince promptly went to work with his best bag of pleas and exhortations. He must have had a direct line to the Almighty that day, for just as the Old South prayers were hitting their climax, in roared a tropical hurricane that turned Boston Harbor and the adjacent ocean into a maelstrom and knocked the French fleet on its beam ends, a swirling shambles of wreckage.

As the poet Henry Wadsworth Longfellow described it years later:

> And even as I prayed
> The answering tempest came;
> It came with a mighty power,
> Shaking the windows and walls,
> And tolling the bell in the tower,
> As it tolls at funerals.
> . . . .
> Down on the reeling decks
> Crashed the o'erwhelming seas:
> Ah, never were there wrecks
> So pitiful as these!

The event was so close to being miraculous that it might well have justified a petition for the beatification of a new saint, St. Thomas of Old South. But the Congregationalists let the opportunity pass.

Anyhow, so much for the power of Old South prayer; there's also much to be said for the power of Old South's voice.

As the pre-Revolution years unrolled, protest meetings at Old South became more and more a symbol of outrage against tyranny, to the extent that eventually the Meeting House dissenters became utterly irksome to Royalists in far-off London. And the feeling was quite mutual.

With James Otis as moderator, Old South meetings in 1768 demanded the removal of British naval guns from Boston Harbor. Later, protests were shouted, loud and long, against the Sugar Act and the high cost of distilling rum, against the Stamp Act and the high cost of feeding British troops, against taxation without representation, against trial without jury by British admiralty courts, against the Townshend Acts and the high cost of drinking tea, and against the perpetrators of the Boston Massacre. It must have seemed to Parliament as though Old South wielded the loudest, most outraged, most clamorous voice in all of North America, which of course it did.

"The Town of Boston," cried a parliamentary grumbler named Venn, "ought to be knocked about their ears and destroyed. You will never meet with proper obedience until you have destroyed this nest of locusts."

But it was the Boston Tea Party itself that gave Old South its finest, most dramatic moment in all those prewar years. That event took place on the night of December 16, 1773, and it played to a packed house.

Seven months earlier, in May, cargo ships of the British East India Company had been turned back at Boston, Philadelphia, and New York with a "Thanks—but at those taxes, who needs tea?" At Annapolis in October, Maryland colonists had greeted a tea shipment with violence. In Charleston, the reaction was the same.

By the time 1773 neared its close, the American colonists were so firmly united in their determination to reject British tea that not an ounce of the stuff could be found for sale on the open colonial market. Meanwhile, the London warehouses of the British East India Company were bulging with 17 million pounds of tea for which there were no teacups—and as far as Bostonians were concerned, no taxes forthcoming.

"Send it to America," ordered the king. And the British, being both stubborn and foolish, designated three ships to be filled with tea cargoes for the Massachusetts Colony.

The first to arrive was the *Dartmouth,* sailing into Boston Harbor on November 28 with 114 tax-tainted chests in her hold. Unfortunately for *Dartmouth's* skipper, he docked his ship at Griffin's Wharf, just a whoop and a sprint from Old South. The action and the timing doomed the ship's cargo before the first mooring line came flying ashore.

During the next two weeks, with the arrival of two more ships, the colonists held stormy meetings at Faneuil Hall and Old South, demanding that the tea be shipped back to London. Such leaders as Jonathan Williams, John Hancock, and Sam Adams kept the crowds so worked up over the issue that on December 16 thousands of irate colonials, unable to cram themselves into nearby Faneuil Hall, adjourned to Old South and bulged its walls with their numbers and their shouted denunciations of King George III. The angry Bostonians, jammed in Old South and overflowing the walks outside, shouted for an end to the tea commerce and the return of all three ships to England.

But the British were adamant. At six o'clock that evening, while Old South waited in candlelight, the final word came to the colonists from the king's representatives: "No return—the tea stays in Boston."

The crowd tensed and went silent. Then Sam Adams got to his feet.

"This meeting can do nothing more to save the country," he declared.

Instantly some 90 men in Indian garb, dressed and painted like Mohawk warriors, tore out of Old South with war cries and tomahawks and led a stampede of enraged Bostonians straight to Griffin's Wharf. There they leaped aboard the ships and spent the next three hours smashing open 342 tea chests and hurling the cargo into the sea. That done, the "Indians" gave a final round of war whoops and vanished with their neighbors, to wash their painted faces and burn their buckskins.

Boston's waterfront on the next day was a tidal bowl of tea leaves that lined the beaches like so much storm-tossed seaweed. Now nothing remained but to sit back and see how London would react.

It took three months for the reaction to get back across the Atlantic. Not the least of the retaliatory measures was the dispatching of four new regiments of British troops to support the two regiments already on duty in Boston. What's more, many of the newcomers were to be quartered in Boston homes. With that announcement, there was no longer any question about whether there'd be a war; the only question was when.

There was no longer any question either about the British punishing Old South; the only decision to make was how.

General John Burgoyne had a good answer for that. In 1775, he drove out the churchgoers and turned the hallowed old place into a riding school for the cavalrymen of the Queen's Light Dragoons.

He ripped out pews and used them for firewood. Then he brought in gravel and dirt and covered the floor, adding crossbars here and there for jump hurdles. All through the siege of Boston in 1775, the horsemen held regular training sessions inside Old South, pounding their way around the riding track and kicking dirt at the cream-colored walls. Meanwhile, their wives and mistresses applauded from the galleries, where wine was served, whiskey was poured, and snuff was sniffed. When George Washington finally drove the British out of Boston in March 1776, one of the first things he did was to pay a visit to Old South, take a look at the mess, and say in effect, "O.K., let's get busy and clean it up."

It remains clean and proud to this day. It has survived the hot air of election sermons delivered by generations of Massachusetts governors. It survived the Great Fire of 1872, when everything around it went down in flames. It survived the indignity of being a temporary United States Post Office following the big fire. It survived the humiliation of being sold at auction in 1876, when it was marked for demolition under an early urban-renewal plan. It was saved from destruction then and bought back by indignant citizens who restored it to grace.

It has caused a lot of trouble through the years, both for itself and its enemies. But it has never knuckled under to injustice.

In other words, it's typical of the people who built it.

And it remains today a shrine to stirring events, the most vivid of which certainly must have been the one that is memorialized by four lines inscribed on a Boston waterfront plaque commemorating the great Tea Party:

> No! Ne'er was mingled such a draught
> In palace, hall or arbor,
> As freemen brewed and tyrants quaffed
> That night in Boston Harbor.

Witch-Bane and Women's Lib

FRIENDS OF JUDGE SAMUEL SEWALL may not have real-
ized it, but when the Boston jurist humbly apologized in Old South
for his part in the Salem witch trials he was dissociating himself
from an age-old sickness of man.

For a time there, back in the 17th-century Bay Colony, the accepted tenets of freedom included the freedom to snare and kill
witches. Self-righteous clerics and judges, eager to make a reputation for themselves, clamored for a chance to lead search-and-destroy
missions, chiefly around the countryside of Salem. These missions became so productive that the prudent thing for any witch-suspect
to do was to point an accusing finger at somebody else and hope to
outshout him or her. "Me? Certainly not! It's my cousin Abby and
her demons. Get her!" And thus the numbers multiplied.

The hysteria of that time shook the lives of many prominent men.
To somebody like Judge Sewall, whose Salem participation had been
a one-shot minor sort of thing, it meant merely the embarrassment
of making a contrite and abject apology, delivered in a plea for
public forgiveness. To someone like the Reverend Cotton Mather,
the most fanatical witch-baiter in American history, it meant the
unforeseen ruination of his most ambitious dream, that of becoming the president of Harvard. He probably could have risen to that

chair if he hadn't been so headstrong and irrational in his pursuit of night-flying broomsticks.

It's not fair, of course, to blame Salem alone for the witch-hunt mania; and Salem, incidentally, has been the victim of bad publicity in this whole business, for despite popular misconceptions, the townspeople never did *burn* a witch, though they did hang 19 and seemed to enjoy watching the executions. Salem, as a matter of fact, was a victim of sorry circumstances that were centuries in the making and that flourished unexpectedly in a favorable Massachusetts climate.

Actually, the whole ugly business can be traced directly back to the Bible and to the exhortation of Exodus XXII: 18—"Thou shalt not suffer a witch to live." Thus, for many centuries, authorities in many lands had approved of witch-killing as standard operating procedure and had quoted the Bible as their warrant to do so.

The witch trials under the Inquisition removed the practice from the ordinary and made it something special. Witch-hunting inquisitors were authorized to obtain confessions, by torture if necessary. The witch who confessed under torture might be condemned to an "easy death"—by hanging or beheading; refusal to confess meant burning at the stake. Gradually the hysteria spread throughout Europe. Pope Innocent VIII gave it a leg up with his papal bull of 1484, decreeing "unprecedented severity" against all witches. When England got caught up in the trend, in the late 1500s, Queen Elizabeth I condemned scores of guiltless women to death by hanging. King James I, who succeeded her in 1603, had written an alarming tome on demonology ten years earlier, and upon coming to the throne, launched a terrible witch-purge of his own. In 1645–46, England had a semiofficial Witch-Finder General, who poked into places where malevolent fiends might be hiding; his name was Matthew Hopkins, and he operated on a bounty system that paid him 20 shillings per witch.

And it was worse elsewhere in Europe. France came up with a judge in Toulouse who arranged to exterminate 400 "witches" at a single mass execution. Another judge in Nancy got rid of 800 in six years. The city of Treves accounted for some 7,000, more or less. Much earlier, France, acceding to the demands of England, had Joan of Arc burned at the stake for heresy and witchcraft. By the time the Inquisition had run its 300-year course, Europe as a whole had executed more than 300,000 women for plain old witchcraft in general. It was a bad climate for women's lib and even for those honest souls who dared to voice sincere doubts about a neighbor's involvement with demons. The reaction too often was "Aha!—she's one herself!"

Inevitably the fever blew across the North Atlantic and touched down in New England. There it began to claim its victims, both male and female, in the 1640s when Massachusetts, Rhode Island, and Connecticut all decreed the death sentence for warlocks and witches. The Connecticut settlers hanged a woman, Alse Young of Hartford, in 1647 and finished off eight more colonists in the next 15 years. Bostonians executed Margaret Jones of Charlestown on a bright June day in 1648. Beautiful, cultured Anne Hibbins, widow of the Bay Colony's former representative to England, was convicted on hearsay evidence and hanged in Boston despite her late husband's eminent reputation.

Thus by 1688, conditions were just right for a wave of terror. And in that year, the Reverend Cotton Mather decided to ride with the tide and capitalize on the excitement. And to make matters worse, he actually believed in the righteousness of his position.

Mather was the Colony's outstanding minister. He was brilliant, learned, sharp, and ambitious. The son of the Reverend Increase Mather, he aspired to the position his father held as president of Harvard. And he mistakenly interpreted the rising witchcraft hysteria as a God-given opportunity for him to glean prestige and popularity while simultaneously leading his followers away from Satan. Obviously, he decided, the thing to do was to impress the public with his dedication and authority by persecuting accused witches wherever and whenever he could find them.

Besides, Mather took witchcraft most seriously. He had read that Anne Hutchinson, who was thought by many to have been a witch, had been guilty of some highly questionable bedroom performances: "Convicted of holding about 30 monstrous opinions at one time, growing big with child, and at length coming to the time of her travail, she was delivered of about 30 monstrous births at once, whereof some were bigger, some were lesser, and none of any human shape." Or so read the records.

And of Anne's cousin, who had also been a witch-suspect, Mather read that she had been "delivered of as hideous a monster as per-

haps the sun ever looked upon. It had no head. The face was below
the breast. The ears were like an ape's, and grew upon the
shoulders. The eyes and mouth stood far out. The nose was hooking
upwards. The breast and back were full of short prickles, like a
thorn-back. The navel, belly, and the distinction of sex, which
was female, were in the place of the hips. The back parts were on
the same side with the face. The arms, hands, thighs, and legs were
as other children's, but instead of toes it had on each foot three claws
with talons like a fowl. Upon the back above the belly, it had a
couple of great holes like mouths, and in each of them stood out
a couple of pieces of flesh. It had no forehead, but above the eyes
it had four horns, two being more than an inch long, hard and
sharp, and the other two somewhat less."

Mather believed all this blather, chiefly because he wanted to.
He even incorporated it into his serious writings. And he not only
believed in witches; he also firmly believed in himself as the Colony's predestined witch-finder.

Accordingly he asked around for a good lead or two and was
advised by informers that the 13-year-old daughter of Mr. and Mrs.
John Goodwin of Boston's North End area was subject to fits that
were apparently of "diabolical origin." When he checked into the
matter, he was overjoyed to discover that the girl's younger brothers
and sisters also showed symptoms of possession. Four, maybe five, in
one family? This was too much for the opportunistic Mather to
resist. He checked into the matter and found the source of the
problem—Goodwife Glover, the family laundress' mother, a sharp-
tongued Irish woman who was frequently heard to speak in a
strange language. Mather promptly persuaded the youngsters to
testify, and poor Mrs. Glover wound up on the end of a Boston
Common gallows rope. Mather was on his way; but unfortunately
for him, he was heading in the wrong direction.

Before the year was out, a hotheaded minister named Samuel
Parris arrived in Salem and leaped enthusiastically into a stew of
local fights and quarrels which had ripped the town apart so badly
that no other minister wanted any share of it. Parris added to the
community's burdens by bringing to live with him two black slaves
from the West Indies, a man named John and his wife Tituba.
And within two years, Tituba was teaching her personal brand of

voodoo and black magic to two impressionable young girls of the town, Ann Putnam and Mercy Lewis.

They learned their lessons well, those girls. They learned to have fits on demand and to mouth weird tongues the like of which Salem had neither seen nor heard. Then they all ganged up to testify to witchcraft charges against Tituba herself, and that was the end of the line for the slave.

While the black woman was in jail awaiting execution, however, she chose not to remain idle. She incriminated two other Salem women, Sarah Osburn and Sarah Good. They in turn put the finger on neighbors Rebecca Nurse and Martha Corey. And this madness kept spreading until more than 100 persons were in prison awaiting death for witchcraft; Gallows Hill in Salem became the popular meeting spot for thousands of people who enjoyed seeing other people get hanged—or in one case, pressed to death.

And Cotton Mather made certain he had a hand in the prosecutions whenever he got the chance.

Following is the death roster of witches and warlocks for the so-called Black Year of 1692 in Salem:

June 10—Bridget Bishop.

July 19—Sarah Good, Elizabeth Howe, Susanna Martin, Rebecca Nurse, Sarah Wildes.

August 19—George Burroughs, Martha Carrier, George Jacobs, John Proctor, John Willard.

Sept. 19—Giles Corey.

Sept. 22—Martha Corey, Mary Easty, Alice Parker, Mary Parker, Ann Pudeator, Wilmot Read, Margaret Scott, Samuel Wardell.

And while they were about it, the Salemites also convicted and hanged two dogs.

Most of the witchcraft victims were convicted on the flimsiest kind of hearsay evidence. Bridget Bishop, for example, was a tavern keeper whose worst fault seemed to be that she was "too ready with her tongue." Or so said her neighbors, who disliked her primarily for her occupation and saw to it that she was accused of sorcery and hanged. Martha Carrier, thrown into jail with four of her children, was convicted solely on the lying testimony of her eight-year-old daughter, who claimed to have been a witch herself since the age of six. This was so ridiculous even to the fanatics that Martha might have won her release except for Cotton Mather's intrusion and his insistence that she be done away with.

Another case that Mather pushed to its gruesome limit was that of George Burroughs, a Harvard graduate and a minister who had an excellent reputation with 20 years' experience in the pulpit. Burroughs had fled from the squabblings of Salem just before the arrival of Samuel Parris and had gone north to Maine to lead a new congregation. He was doing well in his up-country position until the spring of 1692, when Ann Putnam and Mercy Lewis seemed to recall that Burroughs had busied himself with witchcraft before leaving town. As a matter of fact, they added, they had seen him presiding over an orgiastic Witches' Sabbath, held in a lonely Salem meadow. That was enough to warrant sending a posse to arrest him and bring him back to Salem for trial as a warlock. He was sentenced to be hanged at Gallows Hill on August 19.

Throughout the entire affair, Burroughs displayed no emotion whatever until the hangman's noose was actually around his neck. Then, granted a chance for a few last words, he began to pray so ardently and passionately that onlookers were taken aback in wonderment, and some even began to cry out for his release. This abrupt change of mood shocked Cotton Mather into action; he galloped his horse to the front of the crowd, leaped to the gallows platform in front of Burroughs, denounced the minister to the spectators as a pious hypocrite, and warned them that it was an old trick of Satan's to drape himself in piety when the going got rough. The mood of the crowd changed as suddenly as it had before, and Burroughs was hanged.

Another who almost beat the system, and in a way succeeded, was old Giles Corey. This stalwart man, at the age of 80 years, knew enough about the law to realize that if an accused person pleaded guilty to being a warlock, all of his property would be confiscated as soon as he'd been executed. On the other hand, Corey had a pretty good idea that if he pleaded innocent, he was still sure to find hemp around his neck. However, by refusing to plead either way, he could expect to be tortured to death, but the court could not deprive his family of his property. So Corey chose torture.

They laid him on his back and placed a wooden platform upon his body. Then they began to heap heavy stones upon the platform, slowly and one by one, hoping to the very end that the steadily increasing weight would crush his will and force him to cry out his answer. But Corey held out in spite of them; he died under the pressure but aware at the end that his children would not be left in poverty.

Shortly after Corey's death, the hysteria began to taper off both in Salem and in Boston. There were several reasons for this. For one thing, many colonists were getting downright panicky over the realization that they themselves at any moment might wind up as convicted witches solely on the faked testimony of some vituperative neighbor; nobody was safe. For another thing, the public had been made uneasy by the parallel reactions of Samuel Sewall and Nathaniel Saltonstall, both highly respected jurists who had withdrawn in disgust and horror after a single experience at conducting a Salem witch trial. In addition, the authorities themselves were beginning to show doubt as to the wisdom of pressing the persecutions so fervently and in October of 1692 had abolished all "emergency" witch-courts in favor of more stable sittings on the regular court calendar.

But probably the major cause for the change in public opinion was the way in which groundless accusations were being lodged against persons seemingly above suspicion. These were accusations so flagrantly absurd that many judges were refusing to preside at the trials. For example, the Reverend John Hale of Beverly, who had been building a sensational reputation as a witch-finder, came home one night to discover that his own wife had been accused and booked for trial. This was too much for Hale, who promptly turned into a red-hot defender of civil rights and personal liberties.

Equally astounded was Governor Sir William Phips when he was informed that his wife, Lady Phips, had been branded a witch.

Phips, however, was not the sort of a man to frighten easily or to shrink before the ravings of a mob of fanatics. He was one of the most courageous and colorful figures of his day; and perhaps if they had taken the time to consider his background, the accusers would have prudently refrained from hurling witchcraft charges into his home.

Phips was born in a cabin in the Maine woods in 1651. As a youth, he became a shipwright in Boston. In 1674, he married a rich Boston widow whose father had good connections with the

Crown. And he told his bride, "I'll yet be a captain of a king's ship and command better men than I am myself accounted."

He made good on both points. He formed a Boston company to build and finance a trading ship, which provided him with a modest stake and won him access to wealthy circles in London. In 1682, intrigued by tales of shipwrecked Spanish galleons, he decided to chance a career of treasure hunting. In 1686, he teamed with the Duke of Albemarle in forming a London company of "Gentlemen Adventurers" and obtained a patent from King James II to search for treasure. The company had two ships of its own, with Phips commanding one, the *James and Mary*.

Within a year, Phips and his mates found a wreck that had been sought by treasure hunters for half a century. It was the flagship galleon of a Spanish treasure fleet that had gone down in a hurricane while bound from Vera Cruz to Cadiz. It lay in six fathoms of water off Ambrosia Bank, just off the island of Hispaniola. Phips's divers recovered gold, silver, doubloons, and jewels worth more than 300,000 pounds and returned in triumph to London. The adventure made Phips independently wealthy and gained him a knighthood for the success of his voyage and its profit for the Crown.

In London, Phips joined Increase Mather in trying to get a new charter for Massachusetts (the Bay Colony charter had been canceled in 1684). A new charter for the royal colony of Massachusetts was granted in 1691 by William III, who had succeeded James II. Mather, given the authority to nominate all its officers, chose Phips the Governor.

With a background as hardy as his, it was logical that Phips reacted to the charges against his wife by resolving to do all he could to quell the witchcraft hysteria and bring his colonial neighbors to their senses. At the moment, he was busy with military operations against the Indians and French in the north, but he sent word to friends in Boston that he'd be home to put things back in order before there were any more hangings.

Then came another shocker: Warlock charges were lodged against 70-year-old Captain John Alden of Boston, the highly respected son of John and Priscilla Alden of Plymouth Colony. A man with a brilliant record, an old soldier with a reputation for courage and reliability, he was dragged into court. Standing before the bench, he demonstrated his contempt for the whole affair by refusing to remove his hat. When the women who had accused him stood up to testify, he leaped onto a chair. "Let me see them clearly!" he shouted.

As the story of the trial has told it: "There stands Alden, a bold fellow, with his hat on his head before the judges. He sells powder and shot to the Indians and the French, and lies with Indian squaws and has Indian papooses."

But whatever his talents or frailties, Alden was a man who knew how to take care of himself. He was sentenced to be hanged, but he escaped.

And finally came another blockbuster: Cotton Mather's own mother was named a witch.

Mrs. Mather was fortunate; she was shielded by the public reaction that had arisen. The wave of preposterous developments had convinced almost everyone that it was time to take a second look at the tide of hysteria and to temper the rash of hangings. The climate of terrorism cooled almost immediately. There were still more than 150 persons sitting in jail awaiting trial, but concurrently there was a sudden employment dip in the ranks of the executioners.

But Cotton Mather, being hard-nosed and stubborn, saw the reversal in the trend as a rebuke to his standing as the Bay Colony's foremost witch-fighter and as a threat to his dreams of still greater glory. He decided, therefore, that he needed a victory in one more sensational witchcraft case that would pit him directly against Satan to convince the public that the Mather method had been the right one all along. Thus when he heard of the case of Margaret Rule, which came to his attention in September of 1693, he leaped at it with avidity.

Margaret was a Boston girl who lived in the North End. Like so many other girls of her time, she was said to be having fits that were caused by the devil. When Mather went to investigate, he found the girl in bed. She said she was being tortured by "a little black man, a rat and divers imps," who were demanding that she give her soul to Satan. Mather was told that there were ghosts sharing the room with her and that she was causing terrifying sounds in the house. He also got the word that the attendant imps and demons had a habit of raising Margaret to the ceiling and leaving her suspended in air.

This was just the sort of case Mather had been looking for. In fact, it was a bit more than he'd anticipated, and so he called in his father, the Reverend Increase Mather, to help with the "laying on of hands to exorcise the devil."

Father and son thereupon spent six weeks working on Margaret. It was a hard fight. Before it was over, just about everybody in Boston and Salem felt a personal stake in the outcome. And through it all, Margaret's bedroom was a wild arena of prayers, shouts, exhortations, incantations, curses, shrieks, and hallelujahs. People standing in the roadway outside regularly demanded updated reports on which side was ahead and cheered either setbacks or progress, depending upon what they individually thought of Cotton Mather and his tactics.

Then Margaret herself put an end to it all. She announced abruptly that the show was over, that a strange white presence had suddenly appeared to her and had sent all the imps and demons scurrying away. There was no more need for the Mather machinations, Margaret said. She was her own smiling self again, and it was time for everybody to go home.

But what Cotton Mather had hoped would be accepted as a great triumph over the powers of darkness turned almost overnight into a public disgrace. This was brought about by Robert Calef, who had always denounced the witchcraft hysteria and who had publicly branded Cotton Mather as an opportunistic charlatan and faker. Calef reasoned that if he could find some way to drag Mather into court over the Margaret Rule case, Mather could be destroyed.

Calef visited Margaret and talked with her for long hours. He quizzed her and cajoled her, put her through examination and cross-examination, questioned this and probed that, and returned again and again to what Mather had described as facts and proved to his complete satisfaction that they were lies.

Finally, having established in his own mind that both Margaret and Mather had been play-acting, he withdrew. Calef thereupon set to work writing a detailed summary and exposure of the case. With that accomplished, he leaked enough of the document to the public to raise serious questions as to Mather's manner of handling the affair, as to his integrity, as to his distortion of facts, as to his sensational claims versus Margaret's sworn admissions, and even as to what he'd had in mind when he persuaded Margaret to submit to his "laying on of hands"—the massaging of breasts and belly and other bedside familiarities. Then Calef sat back to await the explosion.

It came immediately. Mather reacted precisely as Calef had hoped. He had Calef arrested and thrown into jail on a slander charge. He rolled up his sleeves for a bitter and furious fight that would destroy Calef in court. And then suddenly he realized his terrible mistake; to take the case to court would be to destroy himself. In the end, to salvage his reputation, Mather had to be content with ignoring Calef's accusations. After that, Cotton Mather ceased to matter anymore as a hunter of witches or for that matter as a prospective candidate for the presidency of Harvard.

Finally Sir William Phips came home from the fighting in the north, and in 1693, issued a strong proclamation that freed all the witch-suspects who were still in jail. And the madness at last came to an end.

Years later, in 1706, Ann Putnam, who had given hearsay evidence that had led to several hangings, suddenly showed up in her hometown church and publicly confessed that she had given false testimony. "The devil made me do it," she said in effect.

In retrospect, it is not to be wondered at that the great majority of those who were accused of witchcraft and those who were executed were women. Throughout the ages, the woman has been the symbol of witchcraft, while the man has seemed more or less to wander in and out of the picture by happenstance. Nobody in his right mind would ever report seeing a warlock flying a broomstick. Thus the cases in Salem and Boston against men like Alden, Burroughs, and Corey were in the minority, while the cases against women filled most of the pages.

This, of course, fits in with woman's position in the early days of the Bay Colony and with women's rights; for the most part, they didn't have any.

The one situation in which a woman of those days was given her head was in her dedication to getting herself married. It was conceded that she'd have a hard time trying to make a go of it as a colonial spinster, the Colony as a whole being a man's world. Therefore she was allowed generous leeway in trying to get a husband. She could mingle with the crowds at the hangings and there perhaps get acquainted with some virile young bachelor newly arrived from England. She could accept a party invitation and go unchaperoned. She could run a tavern or a stable or some other enterprise that would attract male customers. She could prod a man into proposing marriage. If she could trick him, fine. And if she chose to single out one man and lay siege to him with letters and flattery, she was free to do so.

Cotton Mather, before his downfall and after the death of his first wife, was besieged in such fashion by a woman who had decided he was just the right man for her and who didn't hesitate to let him know about it. Bemoaning the situation, he wrote: "This young gentlewoman first addressed me with diverse letters and then makes me a visit at my house; wherein she gives me to understand that she has long had a more than ordinary value for my Ministry; and that since my present condition has given her more liberty to think of me, she must confess herself charmed with my person, to such a degree that she could not but break in upon me with her most importunate requests that I would make her mine. What snares she may be laying for me, I know not. Lord help me, what shall I do? I am a miserable man."

Marriage itself, at that time, was a simple enough matter. Rather than run the risk of having any Church of England ceremonies gain a foothold in the Colony, the authorities for almost a century held a ban against church weddings and restricted the rite to a civil pact. Probably few women, if any, objected to this, since the fundamental goal was to get a husband, not a role in a pageant.

On the other hand, a divorce was a rather difficult thing for a man to manage and almost an impossibility for a woman. A man could get rid of his wife if he could prove her guilty of adultery. If a woman tried to get a divorce on similar grounds, though, she'd be treated to a shrug of the shoulders and sent home to cook supper. Not until after the start of the Revolution was there any record of a woman in the Colony winning a divorce just because her husband got caught in bed with somebody else. Any woman determined to get a divorce was out of luck unless she could prove cruelty or lack of support, and even then she might have to tie up the whole package with proof of desertion covering some vague period that might run as long as three years.

The quickest way in which either a man or a woman could win freedom was to be convicted of bigamy. But the sentence for that was not divorce; it was death.

In other words, whether in court or in their own homes, women rarely had any more rights than their men chose to grant to them. They were not supposed to be educated; they were supposed to be full-time housekeepers and breeders of big families. And if they could produce enough children to rent out a few to a neighboring farmer or merchant, so much the better.

A woman who failed to catch a husband was expected to leave the family fireside and go to work as a servant for somebody else; she certainly couldn't expect to be supported at home. If she did get a husband for herself, she could expect to work from dawn to dark, with enough time out, of course, to keep on with the business of becoming pregnant. Meanwhile, there were candles to dip, meals to cook, soap to boil, butter to churn, cloth to weave, clothes to make, beds to warm, fires to feed, fruits to preserve, snakes to kill, babies to nurse, lamps to fill, quilts to patch, vegetables to trade, floors to clean, and once a month a mountain of laundry to take to the creek or to boil in the fireplace and at that get it only halfway clean.

It's little wonder that she was never divorced for adultery; she scarcely had the time.

Changes came, of course, with the passing of the years and the coming of 18th-century prosperity. A woman had it much better by then. She could go to dances, set up a millinery shop, teach domestic arts to children, and clothe herself in new styles that were sent over from London on well-dressed dolls, all daintily outfitted with everything from coats, hats, and shoes to skirts, nightgowns, and underwear. All she had to do was to make her selections, send her order back to London, and then figure out how to get her husband to pay for it.

At such times, perhaps a little witchcraft was in order.

Lion and Unicorn Country

TWO HUNDRED YEARS AGO the cellar of the Old State House in Boston was filled with fine bottled wines; today it is filled with the roar of subway trains.

The wines got there in colonial days by being brought across the Atlantic to the wharves at the foot of King Street and then being hauled uphill for storage in cool, dark bins. The subway got there in 1904 when the city did nothing to protect the Old State House against the encroachments of downtown development and rapid-transit tunnels.

But though its original basement has long since disappeared, the Old State House from the ground up looks much the same as it did, for example, on a dark night back in 1747 when thousands of angry citizens hurled bricks through the windows, protesting the seizure of Yankee sailors to fill the crews of British warships. The British got the message, and the ships sailed away short-handed.

The Old State House looks down on what used to be called Pudding Lane. The top of its east wall is adorned with a lion, a unicorn, and a sundial that has trouble finding the sun. The lion and the unicorn still irritate a lot of Bostonians. We won the Revolution, didn't we? Then let's get those symbols of royalty out of there. Replace them with eagles or ships' figureheads or something else that's pure American.

But the lion and the unicorn remain, reminders to anyone who looks up at them that this is the place where British governors ruled over the Bay State settlers until the colonists in 1775 finally said, "That's enough! Just get along home."

Some 140 years earlier it had become apparent that Boston badly needed a public Town House and a Market Place. Space was available in the Pudding Lane-King Street-Crooked Lane area where public land sloped down toward the waterfront. Here, since 1632, there had been a church of sorts, built of mud walls and a thatched roof. Here too had been a whipping post and also stocks and pillory for the cooling off of wrongdoers and the incidental amusement of the passersby. And probably the sight of no miscreant in the stocks provided the Puritans with more amusement than that of Edward Palmer sitting there; he had designed and built the device and then became the first man sentenced to use it—for demanding an exorbitant fee.

By 1655, the Puritans, though heartily agreeing that a Town House was needed, were heatedly disagreeing about how to pay for the thing. Fortunately for them, one of their wealthiest merchants, Robert Keayne, chose that time to die, leaving a will that is still a Boston record holder for length, running to 54 pages of miniscule script. When they finally deciphered it, the Puritans learned to their delight that Keayne had left Boston 300 pounds toward erecting a wooden Town House with a built-in Market Place, providing that the structure contain a Town Library as well as headquarters space for the Ancient and Honorable Artillery Company, of which he was the charter commander.

Keayne's generosity was totally unexpected, especially since the Town Fathers early on had dragged him into court and fined him 200 pounds for making too much money in his own business. Perhaps he was subtly putting them in their place when he conditioned his bequest with numerous detailed demands on just how the Town House must be built—66 feet long, 36 feet wide, Market Place on the ground floor, meeting room on the second floor extending three feet beyond the ground floor, 21 pillars 10 feet high between the two floors, and a sloping roof with a walk, twin turrets, and railings.

All this was fine with the Puritans. Eagerly accepting Keayne's money, they built their Town House in 1658 and in precisely the way Keayne had specified.

For the next 53 years, the Town House was at the center of a number of crises and dramatic events. It was a working headquarters for the royal governors, the Governor's Council, the deputies of the General Court, the judiciary, and the leading town officials. Its walls echoed the exciting trials of pirates captured at sea, the clanging of weaponry as King Philip's Indian warriors burned their way toward Boston in 1675, the outcries for and against sending Captain Kidd to a London gallows, the uproar over the expulsion of Sir Edmund Andros.

And in between crises, there was a lot of jovial drinking on the premises. As Judge Samuel Sewall observed in his diary on February 6, 1707:

> Queen's Birthday. I could not find it in my heart to
> go to the Town House, because hardly anything is pro-
> fessedly done there but drinking healths.

But if any toasts were ever proposed to the long life of the Town House itself, it was a waste of good rum. A fire in 1711 burned the structure flat to the ground. And while the flames were still raging, a number of opportunistic Bostonians carried to safety and seclusion all the books in the Town Library, which left the community bereft of volumes but greatly enhanced the holdings of private collectors. The Town Fathers later issued an order for all book snatchers to "stand and deliver." But nobody did either.

Within two years, the colonists had built a new Town House on the site of the old. And this time, since it was no longer any affair of Robert Keayne's, they built it of brick and extended its length to 112 feet.

One thing this enlargement of the original structure accomplished was to increase the fuel consumption of the next fire, which occurred on December 9, 1747, and completely gutted the building's interior. The flames destroyed such irreplaceable items as oil portraits of British royalty, original town records, hand-carved furniture, costly hangings, and thousands of bottles of good wine.

As reported in the *Boston Weekly News-Letter:*

"Yesterday morning between 6 and 7 o'clock, we were exceedingly surprised by a most terrible fire, which broke out at the Court House in this town, whereby that spacious and beautiful building, except the bare outward walls, was entirely destroyed.

"As the fire began in the middle or second story, the records, books, papers, furniture, pictures of Kings and Queens, etc., which were in the Council Chamber, the Chamber of the House of Representatives and the apartments thereof in that story were consumed; as also were the books and papers in the offices of the upper story. Those in the offices below were mostly saved. In the cellars, which were hired by several persons, a great quantity of wines and other liquors were lost.

"The public damage sustained by this sad disaster is unexpressibly great, and the loss to some particular persons, 'tis said, will amount to several thousand pounds.

"The vehemence of the flames occasioned such a great heat as to set the roofs of some of the opposite houses on fire, notwithstanding they had been covered with snow, and it was extinguished with much difficulty. How the fire was occasioned, whether by defects in the chimney or hearth as some think, is uncertain."

But at least the fire gave proof that Bostonians certainly were experts at building brick walls. Although nothing else remained of the building, the walls themselves came through the fire in such good shape that they were left standing undisturbed and were used as the walls for a third Town House on the same site. And those are the walls of today's Old State House.

In 1750, shortly after its reconstruction was completed, Captain Francis Goelet described the building in his journal:

"They have also a Town House, built of brick, situated in King's Street. It's a very grand brick building, arch'd all round and two stories high, sashed above. Its lower part is always open, designed as a Change, tho' the merchants in fair weather make their Change in the open street at the easternmost end. In the upper story are the Council and Assembly Chambers, etc. It has a great cupola, sashed round, and which on rejoicing days is illuminated."

It was in this building on December 16, 1761, that the patriot James Otis stood before the Crown's representatives and delivered his fiery outburst against the Writs of Assistance.

No full record of Otis's four-hour speech remains, but it must have been a beauty. The Writs literally were nothing less than no-knock entry permits and blanket search warrants, empowering British revenue officers to storm into any dwelling place or storage warehouse, by day or night, using force if necessary, and to search for any contraband goods that might—or might not—be hidden there. The despotism inherent in any such infamous fishing expedition was so blatantly outrageous that Boston merchants and householders alike rose up with a roar of protest.

The occasion of Otis's speech was truly a history-making moment. As John Adams described it some 50 years later: "Then and there the child Independence was born." Nor did it take "the child" long to mature.

Bostonians joined the Philadelphia and New York merchants in boycotting British goods following the Sugar Act of 1764 and the Stamp Act of 1765. But when the Townshend Acts of 1767 again levied duties on imports and called for a Board of Customs Commissioners to be stationed in Boston, the town took the lead in protesting the measures, with angry mobs harrying the revenue agents.

London, well-versed in the handling of unruly colonials, quietly but quickly began shipping troops to Boston. In October 1768, two regiments from Halifax disembarked at Long Wharf; the following month two more arrived, from Ireland.

By midwinter in 1768-69, Boston was a vast British encampment. Asked to provide quarters for the troops, the town refused. By midwinter a year later, two regiments—two had been removed —of British regulars and a battery of artillery were still sitting on the town, the flanks of the Old State House were guarded by British cannon, and the streets of Boston were seething with enraged colonials and jittery Redcoats. Incidents between the citizenry and the soldiers increased daily—not helped much by the British troops parading, with fife and drum, while the townspeople were attending church services.

It was a perfect setting for trouble. And trouble came on March 5, 1770. It was called the Boston Massacre.

The use of the term "massacre" to describe an incident in which five colonials were killed is still subject to question. By today's standards, it would seem that a similar affair could be handled by three or four Boston police cars and that the death toll might be no more than a footnote to holiday weekend statistics. After more than 200 years, the arguments still go on as to whether the incident marked the first official bloodletting of the Revolution and therefore was of great historical significance or whether it was just a case of a group of colonial hoodlums exercising their freedom to throw snowballs and provoke a fight.

Whichever it was, about eight o'clock on the night of the Massacre, two British soldiers and a small group of citizens got embroiled in a shouting match at a point on King Street just beyond the east wall of the Old State House. As the exchange grew hotter, some unknown person sounded an alarm that brought a band of belligerent colonists rushing to the scene to share in the insults and the excitement. This action isolated a British sentry on duty in front of the nearby guardhouse, and he quickly found himself being pelted by snowballs.

The sentry's yell for help brought eight more Redcoats hurrying out from the guardhouse. This delighted the snowballers, who now had nine targets instead of one and readjusted their barrage accordingly.

The Redcoats responded by fixing bayonets to their muskets. The crowd reacted by adding bricks and stones to its arsenal of missiles. The Redcoats in turn loaded and primed their muskets. The colonials jeered at them and whacked the muskets with sticks.

At this point, with rocks and snowballs and curses filling the air, one of the soldiers took a sharp blow on the head and went down. He jumped up in a rage and fired at the crowd, killing a black man named Crispus Attucks. Immediately, some unidentified Redcoat lost his head and shouted "Fire!" and a volley banged out, killing two more citizens and wounding eight, two of whom died later.

That did it. Alarm bells rang out all over Boston. Men and women by the hundreds rushed to King Street, ready to do battle.

Redcoats by the score hurried to the scene from all over town, until almost the entire Twenty-ninth Regiment was drawn up with muskets primed, facing a mob of at least a thousand howling, fist-waving Bostonians. The Revolution might well have begun at that moment except for the fact that the British wisely and coolly decided to move into marching formation and file back to their barracks. It was the smart thing to do; by midnight, the town was calm and peaceful once again.

In the days that followed, the dead men were escorted to a common grave by a colorful procession of town dignitaries and patriots, many of whom kept shouting vows of vengeance against the British. For a few hours, it appeared that another bloody clash was inevitable. Then, at the insistence of Sam Adams, the two British regiments on duty in the center of the town were hastily withdrawn to a fortress site some distance down Boston Harbor where there would be less chance of their getting embroiled with the citizens. And the nine Redcoats who had been directly involved in the shooting incident were formally booked for a trial to be held in the Town House the following October.

Two of Boston's staunchest patriots, John Adams and Josiah Quincy, took over the role of defense attorneys for the implicated troops and successfully won acquittal for all but two of the group. These two, including the soldier who had killed Attucks, were found guilty of manslaughter and sentenced to be "burnt in the hand in open court and discharged." And so ended the Massacre incident, an affair that almost touched off a war five years ahead of schedule. Today, a ring of cobblestones, near the Old State House, marks the site of the Massacre.

As the formative events of the Revolution took shape and the British grudgingly evacuated Boston to fight in the field, the Town House kept pace with history and moved toward its transition to State House. On July 18, 1776, thousands of citizens gathered in King Street below the east balcony to hear the first public reading in Boston of the Declaration of Independence. And that night they celebrated by tearing down all royal emblems, including the lion and the unicorn, and burning them in a great public bonfire. It was another century or so before the reproductions of the beasts were placed on the building.

John Hancock had his big moment there in 1780, when he

was inaugurated as the first Governor of the Commonwealth of Massachusetts. Another gala affair took place in 1782, when Bostonians staged a lavish reception in honor of the French fleet and army, and the wine and rum flowed like water in a millrace. And one year later there was another celebration, when thousands assembled to hear the reading of the Treaty of Paris, ending the Revolutionary War. Then in 1789, George Washington arrived for a reception in his honor and stood on a specially constructed balcony at the west end of the building to review a long procession of troops and Boston tradesmen.

Finally, on July 11, 1798, Governor Increase Sumner stepped out at the head of a lengthy parade of Commonwealth officials and led a march through the streets of Boston to take possession of the new State House, just completed on Beacon Hill. Behind them, they left the Old State House, silent and empty.

The years that followed gave the old structure little to be proud about. The Commonwealth wanted to sell the place and split the money with the town. The town rejected this idea, bought sole title to the property, and then leased it bit by bit to a collection of cobblers, harness makers, wig dealers, wine vendors, and just about anybody else who could afford the rent, no matter what their business.

The United States Bank tried to buy the building for a branch office in 1822, but the town refused to sell. The Washington Monument Commission in 1826 wanted to tear it down and replace it with a statue of George Washington on a horse, but again the town said no. In 1830, the building was renovated and became a City Hall. In 1844, the city government moved out, and the merchants began to move back in. By the late 1870s, it had become a hodgepodge of shops and business offices, plastered with signs and advertisements, and was such a public eyesore that it seemed almost certain to be razed.

Quite possibly this would have happened, except for the fact that the city of Chicago then stepped into the picture with a formal offer to buy the structure, tear it down, move it brick by brick to the shore of Lake Michigan, and reconstruct it there as a national shrine "for all America to revere."

Red-faced Bostonians found Chicago's proposal altogether too humiliating to swallow. As a result of this reaction, the Boston Antiquarian Club was organized, and by 1881, incorporated as the Bostonian Society, it had managed to persuade the Boston Common Council to save the old building and to restore it as nearly as possible to its original design and condition. The society retains custody of the building to this day.

And the lion and the unicorn are right back where they started, along with the sundial that seldom finds the sun.

Pigeons may be pests on Boston Common
today, but at one time, the Animal Rescue
League provided employees who fed the birds
daily. Now the problem is to correct that
mistake.

Atop Beacon Hill stands the State House
with its golden dome. The structure is one of
Charles Bulfinch's masterpieces.

Beacon Hill at night (right),
sloping down toward the Charles River.

Park Street Church, on "Brimstone Corner," lifts its steeple high above the trees of Boston Common.

King's Chapel (right) on Tremont Street. Adjacent to the chapel, on the left, is the burial ground. The obelisk monument to Chevalier de St. Sauveur is in the center.

Granary Burying Ground (below). Here are the graves of John Hancock, Samuel Adams, Paul Revere, and the victims of the Boston Massacre.

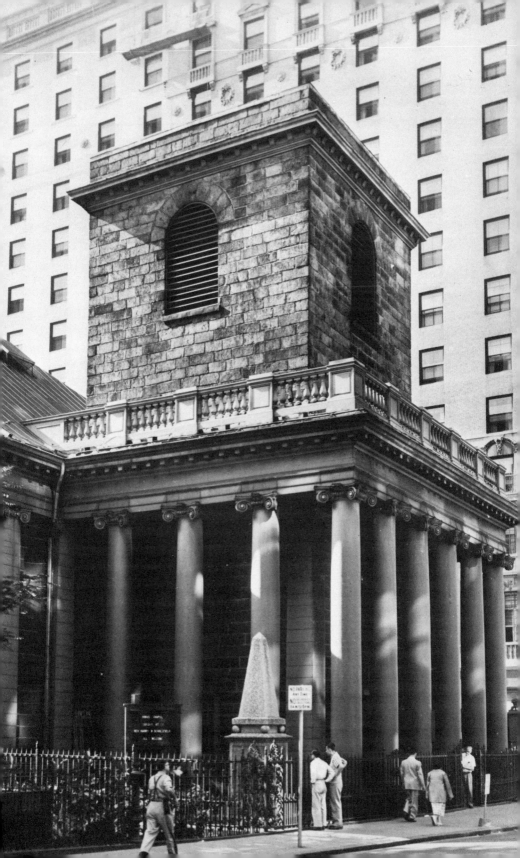

The Old Corner Book Store
(above) is maintained by the *Boston
Globe* and Historic Boston, Inc., as a
memorial to the famous literary
figures of the 19th century who
gathered there, among them
Longfellow, Emerson, Lowell,
Whittier, and Hawthorne.

This restored schoolroom (left)
is typical of those of the early 1760s.

Old City Hall and site of first
public school in the United States.

The statue of Benjamin Franklin
stands on the lawn of the Old City
Hall. On the pedestal are bronze
tablets depicting the important
events in Franklin's life.

The Old State House. From its balcony, the Declaration of Independence was first read to the citizens of Boston.

The Old South Meeting House (left) was both a church and a town meeting house. Around the corner is the site of Benjamin Franklin's birthplace.

Plaque commemorating the Boston Tea Party.

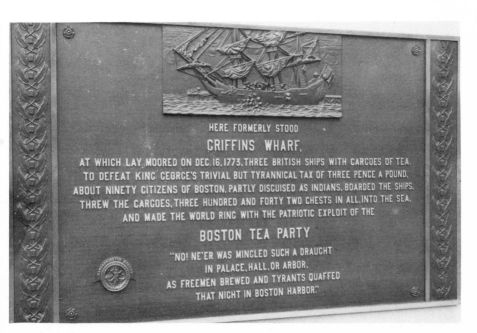

HERE FORMERLY STOOD

GRIFFINS WHARF,

AT WHICH LAY MOORED ON DEC. 16, 1773, THREE BRITISH SHIPS WITH CARGOES OF TEA.
TO DEFEAT KING GEORGE'S TRIVIAL BUT TYRANNICAL TAX OF THREE PENCE A POUND,
ABOUT NINETY CITIZENS OF BOSTON, PARTLY DISGUISED AS INDIANS, BOARDED THE SHIPS,
THREW THE CARGOES, THREE HUNDRED AND FORTY TWO CHESTS IN ALL, INTO THE SEA,
AND MADE THE WORLD RING WITH THE PATRIOTIC EXPLOIT OF THE

BOSTON TEA PARTY

"NO! NE'ER WAS MINGLED SUCH A DRAUGHT
IN PALACE, HALL, OR ARBOR,
AS FREEMEN BREWED AND TYRANTS QUAFFED
THAT NIGHT IN BOSTON HARBOR."

The BLOODY MASSACRE perpetrated in King—Street BOSTON on March 5th 1770, by a party of the 29th

Engrav'd Printed & Sold by PAUL REVERE BOSTON

Faneuil Hall (above), as viewed from across Dock Square.

Paul Revere's famed, but inaccurate, engraving (left) of the Boston Massacre, 1770.

A ring of cobblestones near the Old State House marks the site of the Boston Massacre.

The Paul Revere House (right), built about 1677, is the oldest in Boston. It was Revere's home for 30 years— from 1770 to 1800.

Interior of Old North Church.

Sculptor Cyrus Dallin's statue of Paul
Revere graces the entrance to the Paul Revere
Mall, with famed Old North Church in
the background.

Copp's Hill Burying Ground, in Boston's North End. Here the British mounted a battery of cannon and fired across the harbor at Charlestown during the Battle of Bunker Hill.

U.S.S. *Constitution* sails down Boston Harbor on a "turn around cruise" in 1971.

The Bunker Hill Monument, actually on Breed's Hill in Charlestown, marks the spot of the battle that took place on June 17, 1775. The cornerstone was laid by the Marquis de Lafayette.

Here on the Commonwealth Avenue Mall,
Back Bay, sits a statue of William Lloyd
Garrison, famed for his antislavery speeches
which were first heard in the Park Street
Church.

A "Cradle" Called Faneuil

WITHOUT THE LAVISH GENEROSITY of Peter Faneuil, Boston would not have had a Faneuil Hall. And the Revolution would not have had its "Cradle of Liberty," at least, not at its present location.

But without a strange anti-female quirk on the part of Peter's uncle, Andrew Faneuil, young Peter probably never would have had the money to pay for the Hall in the first place.

Uncle Andrew was one of the million or so Huguenots who fled France in 1685 to get away from the harsh bigotries of King Louis XIV. In his flight, he stopped off in Holland long enough to get married and then crossed the Atlantic to Boston. His wife, said to have been exceedingly beautiful and cultured, died in the Massachusetts Colony in 1724.

Between the riches he brought with him from Europe and the money he eventually made as a Boston merchant, Uncle Andrew became a very wealthy man. He also developed a peculiar hang-up about marriage. For some unexplained reason, the two factors of merchandising and matrimony created circuits of conflict in his mind. The result was that one day old Andrew and young Peter had a conversation which may have gone something like this:

"Peter, take a look at all my ships and shops and shillings."

"Yes sir, Uncle Andrew."

"Quite a pile, eh?"

"Oh yes, sir. Big."

"Some day when I die, this will all be yours, but . . . . . "

"Mine?"

"Don't interrupt, boy. Yours, on one condition."

"What's that?"

"Never get married."

If Peter thought Uncle Andrew a bit daft, he never let on. Not with all that money at stake. He promised to stay single. Thus when he was 38 years old, in 1738, he came into his uncle's fortune. Combined with the wealth he had already accumulated for himself in foreign trade and shipping, this made Peter one of Boston's foremost entrepreneurs.

"The topmost merchant in all the town," John Hancock said. And so he was.

He was also the topmost host in all the town. Peter's philosophy about money was that the stuff should be kept in constant circulation and should provide pleasure for one's good friends. With his sister as hostess and housekeeper, he showed Bostonians what it was like to enjoy first-class living with an 18th-century jet set. His doors were always open. His parties were frequent and brilliant. His Madeira wine and Medford rum punch were the best in Boston. On many a night when the rest of the town was dark and asleep, Peter's home was shining with the bright light of candles and oil lamps and vibrating with the sounds of music and party making.

Though Peter played hard, he also worked hard. He was involved in shipbuilding and in so many other financial deals that he often found it difficult to be in the right place at the right time. And he noticed that various other Boston merchants were having similar problems.

What the town needed, he decided, was a large central market house, preferably in Dock Square right on the waterfront, so designed and laid out as to serve all manner of business needs with a minimum of walking. And if the town felt that such a project would be too expensive, he'd handle it himself.

In July 1740, he made known his proposition in a public statement, offering at his own expense "to erect and build a noble and complete structure or edifice to be improved for a market for the sole use, benefit and advantage of the town . . . ." Some objection came from various quarters, particularly from Boston housewives, who protested that they'd much rather buy from peddlers at their doorsteps than walk all the way to a market.

Work on the "noble structure" began on September 8, 1740. It became a "complete structure" on September 10, 1742. Its market stalls and exchange booths faced out on all four sides— toward the waterfront, the fish market, the hay market, and the sheep market.

Almost as an afterthought, Peter had directed that an extra story, to serve as a meeting hall, be added atop the market area of the structure. The grateful Boston merchants voted to name this place Faneuil Hall. Ironically, the first public use of the Hall was for a memorial service in honor of Peter, who died in March 1743.

Faneuil Hall quickly became Boston's most popular meeting place. Merchants, idlers, shoppers, traders, orators, politicians, pickpockets, shipowners, and sailing masters—all soon discovered that this was where the action was. It became such a necessary part of Boston's daily life that when it was destroyed by fire in 1761, plans for reconstruction were under way even before the smoke had drifted out to sea. The structure was rebuilt within a year, and the meeting hall was enlarged. In 1805–1806, the building was widened, and a third story was added by architect Charles Bulfinch, but the original plan and structure remained.

From the day of its opening, Faneuil Hall became the place to go for anybody interested in hearing the raw opinions of American orators and patriots. Many of the stirring and emotional events connected with the rebellion against the Crown had their origins here. John Hancock and Sam Adams frequently used the Faneuil Hall rostrum to cry out against British oppression. Here the Stamp Act was denounced, and its repeal celebrated. Here on November 5, 1773, patriots held the first of their several Tea Party rallies. Here the portraits of British statesmen sympathetic to the American cause were hung in the corridors and were destroyed when the occupying British used the place for a barracks and a theater in 1775. And here George Washington, as President, was guest of honor at a great banquet in 1789.

Ever since colonial workmen topped off the structure in 1742, its cupola has been surmounted by a huge copper weather vane in the form of a gilded grasshopper, designed by artificer Deacon Shem Drowne. This has always puzzled historians, who see no connection whatever between grasshoppers and Boston. Why not a sea gull? they ask. Or a codfish? Or a blunderbuss? Or a frigate? Why a grasshopper?

Nobody had bothered to explain the grasshopper weather vane in the first place, so nobody can answer the question today. Some historians have tried to make a case out of the fact that there's also a grasshopper weather vane atop the Royal Exchange in London, placed there at the instigation of the British financier and founder of the Exchange, Sir Thomas Gresham. But what this might have to do with Boston and Peter Faneuil is a mystery.

Perhaps Ralph Waldo Emerson had the right explanation. He once pointed out that a grasshopper's ability to slip from one ignominious form into another form equally ignominious was symbolic of the nature of many politicians who have ranted and raved in the Faneuil Hall forum.

Like its decorative cousin the Sacred Cod, however, the Faneuil Grasshopper isn't always secure in its proper place. For example, it suddenly disappeared from public view just after the Christmas holiday period of 1973, much to the dismay of concerned Bostonians.

Its absence went unnoticed until January 4 when Faneuil Hall caretaker Donald MacDonald went to the top of the building on a routine flag-raising chore. To his astonishment, he discovered the cupola weather-vane mast was bare. No grasshopper! And no way of telling how or when it had been removed.

This posed a mystery. How could anyone scale a rounded cupola and lift off a 4-foot, 39-pound metal ornament?

"It would be impossible to carry something that size off the roof," said Boston police detective Paul Revere Carroll. "You'd have to be a monkey just to get up there. Could have been a helicopter." But impossible or not, the weather vane was gone— an item estimated by city officials to be worth $300,000.

State police and city detectives promptly launched an all-points search that spread throughout New England, spilled over into nearby states, and incidentally uncovered an active underworld ring specializing in weather-vane heists. Two copper eagles were recovered, but no grasshopper.

By January 8, however, police had made contact with a tipster in the person of a South Shore steeplejack, who happened to be under arrest on narcotics charges. He proposed a deal. Thus on January 10, a search party scaled a series of tall steel ladders to a point high inside the Faneuil Hall belfry. And there they found the missing grasshopper, hidden under a pile of old flags.

The recovery story led the city's television newscasts that night. And all good Bostonians approved.

"There will be no criminal charges," said the Boston police. "We're just happy to have the thing back. The Hall wasn't the same without it."

Today the oldest tenant of Faneuil Hall is the Ancient and Honorable Artillery Company, which moved from its quarters in the Town House on April 7, 1746. This organization, founded as a "School for Officers and Nursery for Soldiers," now maintains an armory, museum, and headquarters area on the top floor of the Hall. As a unit, the Company has no battlefield record; but its individual members through the years have fought in every war in American history and four times have brought home the nation's highest military decoration, the Medal of Honor. And incidentally, its membership has included four United States Presidents: James Monroe, Chester Alan Arthur, Calvin Coolidge, and John F. Kennedy.

Oddly, the Company's museum displays portraits or photographs of all past commanding officers except the gentleman who originally got the outfit started in 1637, Captain Robert Keayne. Nobody has any idea what he looked like.

In the early days, the Company was considered so important to community life that the Colony passed a law forbidding the holding of a town meeting or any other important event on any day set apart for the Ancients' training.

Even today, the members are still exempt from jury duty. Who'd want to risk an Indian raid or a British bombardment, with an Ancient or two sitting stranded in a jury box?

As a sounding board for political polemics and a catch-all for the gossip of tradespeople, Faneuil Hall quickly became Boston's most active news center. Any person interested in the latest version of the latest rumor had only to walk to the Hall and wander among the crowded stalls to bring himself up-to-date on current events. And if he didn't like the version he heard from the eelmonger, he could slip around the corner and try for a better one from the tinker.

The brick walls of the Hall therefore became a logical posting place for Boston broadsides—printed newssheets and handbills that were pasted up wherever crowds gathered and that served much the same purpose as today's TV newscasts.

These broadsides were abundant, but they were seldom dull. They were as necessary a medium of communication as the town crier, and they were far more informative and entertaining. Everybody read them. Monday's broadside might give the latest information on a boost in bounties for dead pirates. Tuesday's might be a description of an escaped slave—"26 years of age, pretty slender, wearing a gray hat with a clasp on it, breeches of a brownish color, worsted stockings, a periwig of bright brown hair . . . ." Wednesday's might be an official order on what to do about smallpox—"Hang out on a pole at least six feet in length a red cloth, not under one yard long and half a yard wide, from the most public part of the infected house, or be fined 50 pounds and punished by whipping, not to exceed 30 stripes."

A typical Faneuil Hall broadside was one that appeared on March 5, 1772, displaying Paul Revere's classic engraving of the Boston Massacre. Its purpose was not only to recall that specific event to the public mind but also to remind the public that a Boston teenager named Christopher Seider had been killed 11 days before the Massacre by an informer named Ebenezer Richardson who "Remains UNHANGED!!!"

The notice read:

AMERICANS!

BEAR IN REMEMBRANCE

THE HORRID MASSACRE!

Perpetrated in King Street, Boston,

New England

On the Evening of March the Fifth, 1770

When FIVE of your fellow countrymen,

GRAY, MAVERICK, CALDWELL, ATTUCKS
and CARR

Lay wallowing in their Gore!

Being basely, and most inhumanly

M U R D E R E D !

And SIX others badly wounded!

By a Party of the XXIXth Regiment,

Under the Command of Capt. Tho. Preston

REMEMBER!

That Two of the Murderers

Were convicted of MANSLAUGHTER!

By a Jury of whom I shall say

NOTHING!

Branded in the hand!

And dismissed.

The others were ACQUITTED!

And their Captain PENSIONED!

Also

BEAR IN REMEMBRANCE

That on the 22d Day of February, 1770,

The infamous

EBENEZER RICHARDSON, Informer

And tool to Ministerial hirelings

Most barbarously

M U R D E R E D

C H R I S T O P H E R   S E I D E R

An innocent youth!

Of which crime he was found guilty

By his country

On Friday April 20th, 1770;

But remained UNSENTENCED

On Saturday the 22d Day of February, 1772,

When the GRAND INQUEST

For Suffolk County
Were informed, at request,
By the Judges of the Superior Court
That EBENEZER RICHARDSON'S Case
Then lay before his Majesty.
Therefore said Richardson
This day, MARCH FIFTH! 1772
Remains UNHANGED!!!
Let these things be told to Posterity!
And handed down
From Generation to Generation
Till Time shall be no more!
Forever may AMERICA be preserved,
From weak and wicked monarchs,
Tyrannical Ministers,
Abandoned Governors,
Their Underlings and Hirelings!
And may the
Machinations of artful, designing wretches
Who would *ENSLAVE* This People
Come to an end,
Let their NAMES and MEMORIES
Be buried in eternal oblivion,
And the PRESS,
For a SCOURGE to Tyrannical Rulers
Remain FREE.

And an accompanying poem said, in part:

Oh! sword of vengeance, fall thou on the race
Of those who hinder justice from its place.
Oh Murd'rer! Richardson! with their latest breath
Millions will curse you when you sleep in death!

Infernal horrors sure will shake your soul
When o'er your head the awful thunders roll.
Earth cannot hide you, always will the cry
Of Murder! Murder! haunt you till you die!
To yonder grave! with trembling joints repair,
Remember, Seider's corpse lies mould'ring there;
There drop a tear, and think what you have done!
Then judge how you can live beneath the Sun.

Thousands read the piece. It was never recorded that Ebenezer demanded equal time.

Poetry played a part also in a broadside that was pasted to the wall of Faneuil Hall just after the violent Boston earthquake of November 18, 1755. In this one, a versifier named Jeremiah Newland put together 49 stanzas of bad writing to interpret the significance of what had happened and to urge God not to repeat the performance:

Thy terrible Hand is on the Land
    by bloody War and Death;
It is because we broke thy Laws
    that thou didst shake the Earth . . .

We see, O Lord, that thou hast jarred
    most every Habitation;
By that we know thou'rt strong enough
    to sink the whole Creation . . .

Then give us Space and give us Grace,
    that we may give thee Praise;
We know not but we shall be sunk
    in less than forty Days.

The poem worked. Boston did not sink.

To the Old North End

A POPULAR EXPLANATION for the narrow, crooked streets that wander through downtown Boston today is that they were laid out to follow old cow paths. And probably many of them were.

Regardless, all of them today make up a jaywalker's dream of bliss, and the Boston police have long since accepted the fact that the pedestrian lights blinking "WALK" and "DONT WALK" might as well be written in Arawak shorthand. No true Bostonian pays them the slightest attention.

Whatever their origin, the streets first came into official recognition on May 3, 1708, when the Town Fathers posted a lengthy broadside informing the public that "the Streets, Lanes and Alleys of this town are as followeth . . . ."

The colorfully named walkways and roadways that were then listed, with explanations of where they led and why they sometimes curved in on themselves, makes one feel regretful that most such imaginatively designated signposts have long since vanished from the city's street corners.

There were, to mention a few: Frog Lane, leading "from the bottom of the Common, southerly down to the sea"; Flounder Lane, leading from the sea to the town ropewalk; Sentry Street, leading from Beacon Street, past Madam Shrimpton's pasture, and up to

Sentry Hill; Turn Again Alley, leading from the Common past Madam Usher's house; Crab Lane, leading from Castle Tavern in Mackeril Lane, past Mr. Halloway's wharf, and thence to the sea; Elbow Alley; Salutation Alley; Damnation Alley; White Bread Alley; Coin Court; Beer Lane.

And spotted along the way were the numerous pubs and taverns of the times: The Green Dragon, The Bunch of Grapes, The Bell and Bowl, The Black Pig, The Blue Tide, The Red Lion, The Clam and Claw.

Almost directly upon leaving Faneuil Hall, the modern Freedom Trail angles into a number of these old byways and passes alongside the doorsteps and thresholds of buildings that were familiar structures in Boston's most hectic pre-Revolution days and for many years before that.

On Union Street close by Faneuil Hall, for example, is the Union Oyster House or Ye Olde Oyster House or Ye Olde Original Oyster House—whatever you prefer to call it. In any case, it has been serving shucked oysters and cold ale across the same U-shaped mahogany bar since 1826, but it had a lively pre-oyster existence long before that.

Unfortunately there are no records to tell just how ancient the old Oyster House building may be. Union Street itself was laid out in 1636. It was defined in the 1708 broadside as "leading from Platt's corner, passing northwesterly by the Sign of the Dragon, to the Mill Pond." The first reference to the Oyster House building came in 1742, when it was listed as the Union Street property of a Boston merchant named Thomas Stoddard.

Stoddard bequeathed the property to his daughter Patience and her husband, Hopestill Capen, and it eventually became the business headquarters of Thomas Capen, an importer of silks and fancy dress goods. He called the place "At the Sign of the Cornfields."

From 1771 to the time when the Revolutionary shooting began in 1775, the building was the home of the newspaper *Massachusetts Spy*, produced by publisher Isaiah Thomas under the motto "Open to all parties, but influenced by none." When the fighting began, Isaiah felt sufficiently influenced to move his paper to Worcester.

During the Revolutionary War period, the building became the headquarters of Ebenezer Hancock, brother of John Hancock and a paymaster for the Continental Army. George Washington visited there in those days, perhaps to straighten out his expense account.

Somewhat later the house became the temporary home of Louis Philippe, who was to become ruler of France from 1830 to 1848. He eked out his exile in Boston by teaching French verbs to would-be linguists in his second-floor bedroom.

As to its long and popular association with oysters, the establishment has this to say of itself on its menu:

"The great of Boston were familiar sights in Union Street and behind the small-paned windows of the bar. Their coat tails hung down from the high bar stools, and they polished off oysters and clams, crabs and lobsters, quahogs, shrimp and mussels by the million, consuming schooner loads of fish every week and on banner days as many as thirty-five barrels of Cape Cod's finest and most succulent Cotuits. Daniel Webster was a constant customer. He drank a tall tumbler of brandy and water with each half dozen oysters and seldom had less than six plates."

Small wonder he was such a matchless and thunderous orator. "Massachusetts, there she stands! More oysters, Joe."

Just a few yards away on Salt Lane, near the corner of Creek Square, stands the Ebenezer Hancock House, the oldest brick building in Boston. Conveniently, it is just across the alley from the rear entrance to the old Bell in Hand Tavern.

The Hancock House was originally owned and occupied in 1660 by one William Courser, who entered the history books by becoming the first Town Crier of Boston. In 1737, it became the property of James Davenport, a brother-in-law of Benjamin Franklin's, who had long since departed south for Philadelphia.

John Hancock bought the place in 1764 and held ownership until 1785, when he sold it to his brother Ebenezer. John may have occupied the house from time to time but certainly not for any long-term residence. The place to find him was at the mansionlike home he had built for himself on Beacon Hill, adjacent to where the new State House now stands.

There on the Hill, he lived a plush life and entertained lavishly, first as a loud-voiced leader of rebels and later as the distinguished first Governor of the Commonwealth. He was a Hill resident on the night in 1782 when he gave a great banquet for officers of the French fleet and ran out of milk for his punch bowls; whereupon he sent his servants hustling across the road to Boston Common to steal milk from his neighbors' cows, an act which his neighbors roundly applauded in the name of hospitality. He was also a Hill resident on the autumn night in 1789 when he refused to pay a courtesy visit to George Washington at the Old State House, contending that it was the President's obligation to climb Beacon Hill and call on the Governor. George won that showdown. Hancock had expected to be named commander in chief of the Continental Army and never got over the slight when the job went to Washington.

Anyhow, if Hancock ever spent much time in his Salt Lane house, it was probably just to collect the rent or because he was too tired to make it up Beacon Hill to his own bed.

Here at the Salt Lane corner, incidentally, stands the Boston Stone. This consists of a huge stone ball and a stone trough, brought over from England as a paint mill about 1700. In its original use, the ball was rolled back and forth in the trough to grind out oil and pigment. It constituted probably the earliest implement of the paint industry in America—Indians excepted. In its later use, the stone was permanently emplaced to serve as the zero point from which all distances from Boston were measured.

From here on, the Freedom Trail heads directly into Boston's North End, once a favored residential area for colonial patriots, now a warm and friendly reminder of old Italy.

To walk along Salem Street and its neighboring alleys on a sunlit day during marketing hours is almost like being transported to Naples. Crowds swarm along the narrow way, moving from side to side and shop to shop and pushcart to pushcart. Broad trays of squid and shrimp and smelt glisten brightly in the sunshine. The air is rich with the smell of peppers and olive oil, coffee and wine, fresh fruit and cheese.

Strange foods hang in the doorways and in the market windows: giant white rabbits, suspended head downward; geese with their feathers unplucked; huge slabs of tripe.

Music comes from the open shop windows and blends with the cries of the vendors and the loud arguments of the shoppers. Bakery counters are racked with terraced wedding cakes and massive loaves of fresh bread. Fruit stands are polished patterns of red cherries and oranges and bananas and grapes. A nearby drugstore advertises leeches for sale. There are miles upon miles of spaghetti and end-less rivers of tomato sauce. There are sparkling wines and sharp odors of herbs and the sloshing of live eels in a barrel.

Almost always the streets are made gay with colorful decorations hung overhead, either left over from last month's religious festival or fresh ones that have been strung out for the next celebration. And there are tiny American flags and Italian flags in window after window.

There are also signs that advertise a Freedom Trail Haircut, a Freedom Trail Shoeshine, and even a Freedom Trail Submarine Sandwich, whatever that may be. But even such incongruities can't rob the North End of its allure. American or Italian, colonist or citizen, those who have learned to know it have always hated to leave it.

A North End resident, one William Bank, wrote to a clergyman friend in 1776, with reference to his immediate neighbors:

"Our General Court has voted to raise another regiment. The men are backward about enlisting for service, however, as they may be ordered to New York or elsewhere far from home."

To the North End Bostonian, now as then, even that part of the city only five alleys away is a place that's far from home. A man appreciates the freedom to stay put.

But even though some North End patriots may have preferred to do their fighting close to home, Boston and Massachusetts as a whole gave far more than a fair share of men to the ranks of the Conti-nental Army; the figures, in fact, are quite out of proportion, especially since most of the battles were fought south of New England.

For example, during the seven years of war, there were 21 major generals in the army; and 6 of them were from Massachusetts. There were 49 brigadier generals; 10 from Massachusetts. In 1775, there were 37,363 men in the army; 16,499 from Massachusetts. In 1777, the army had 68,720 men under arms; 12,591 from Massachusetts. And so it went throughout most of the war. Even in 1781, when almost all the fighting was in the South and there were 18,006 men in the field, there were 4,423 from Massachusetts to 2,204 from Virginia. Of the total number of troops—231,000—who fought in the Continental Army, Massachusetts supplied 67,000.

As Daniel Webster proclaimed in the United States Senate in

1830: "The bones of her [Massachusetts] sons, fallen in the great struggle for independence, now lie mingled with the soil of every State, from New England to Georgia; and there they will lie forever."

So despite the misgivings of William Bank, there were indeed many Bostonians who fought for freedom on distant battlefields and who came home in gladness to the old North End.

Paul Revere at Large

LIKE THE OLD STATE HOUSE and Faneuil Hall, the Paul Revere House stands today on the site of a building that was destroyed by fire.

The dwelling that is now a popular feature of the Freedom Trail was built on the ashes of the home of the Reverend Increase Mather, which went up in flames in 1676. Thus it was already a familiar old landmark for Bostonians by the time Paul Revere bought it nearly a century later, in 1770. Paul must have had a shrewd and winning way when talking to Boston bankers; he took title to his home for a mere 53 pounds, 6 shillings, and 8 pence in cash, with a mortgage for 160 pounds.

The house is in the heart of Boston's old North End. It faces southeastward on a slope that must have provided the Reveres with a magnificent view of Boston Bay. Today, of course, that view is blocked by tenements, shops, and spaghetti parlors.

The crowded confines of the neighborhood, however, do nothing to lessen the charm of the dwelling's interior. It is furnished today in much the same fashion as when it was called home by the first Mrs. Revere and her eight children, and following that lady's death, by the second Mrs. Revere and another set of eight.

It is a typical colonial two-story dwelling with a second-story overhang. Entry today is by way of the kitchen doorway, which overlooks a pleasing courtyard complete with an iron hand pump. The huge kitchen fireplace, fashioned of brick, is said to be equipped exactly as it was when the Reveres lived there. The kitchen also contains such interesting items as a handmade cradle, an English piggin, a toddy warmer, a cheese press, saddlebags and pistols, and the iron stake Paul used for tethering his cow on Boston Common—which was quite a far hike for a cow.

In the adjoining living room is a fireplace even larger than the one in the kitchen. It is, in fact, big enough to allow a man to sit inside by the flames and roast an ox, if he could stand the heat.

A narrow steep staircase leads to an upper bedroom with still another fireplace and to an annex workroom with yet a fourth fireplace. The Reveres were going to stay warm, no matter what the weather. And with all those children to gather wood, it was no problem to keep all those fireplaces going.

The windows of the house are formed of leaded diamond-shaped panes. And history relates that Paul frequently used his second-story windows to disseminate political propaganda in the form of stark illustrations pasted to the glass. For example, on the first anniversary of the Boston Massacre, he decorated the panes with pictures so striking as to "halt passersby with solemn silence, their countenances covered with a melancholy gloom." One window pictured the ghost of the slain young Christopher Seider "with one of his fingers in the wound, endeavoring to stop the blood . . . ." Paul's accompanying inscription read: *"Seider's pale ghost fresh bleeding stands, and vengeance for his death demands!"* An adjoining window showed Redcoats firing away at the Boston Massacre crowd, with the dead and wounded bleeding all over the ground. *"FOUL PLAY!"* was Paul's inscription for that one.

Aside from such gruesome displays, Paul's house gives every appearance of having been a most pleasant and comfortable place in which to live. One wonders, though, what it was like to have all those little Reveres romping around on a rainy day.

As for the man himself, Paul appears to have been a genius with so many talents and skills—artist, soldier, equestrian, dentist, inventor, silversmith, builder, merchant, mechanic, politician, engineer, dispatch rider—that it seems he might well have become a profitable one-man colony all by himself, if Britain had seen fit to develop him. The Americans, though, knew a good thing when they saw it: Need a man for the job? Get Revere.

Revere's father was a French Huguenot, Apollos de Revoire, who arrived in the Bay Colony from the island of Guernsey and soon established himself as a successful goldsmith and silversmith. Paul was born in Boston on January 1, 1735. He was still a young man when he inherited his father's business and quickly gained the reputation of being the best silversmith in the colonies.

Meanwhile, he kept branching out in so many other different directions that it's a wonder he ever had time to make his exquisite silver bowls and pitchers.

For example, he closed up his shop during the French and Indian War and took off at the age of 20 to serve as an artillery lieutenant. He became a co-organizer of the first Scottish Rite Masonic Lodge in the Colony. He gained such a high reputation as a horseback rider and horse trader that the patriots' Committee of Safety kept him forever galloping in and out of Boston on messenger duties; when the Thirteen Colonies were organizing for war, he was practically a commuter.

Shortly after his famous midnight ride to Lexington, he became the engraver and printer responsible for making and issuing the Patriots' paper currency. He learned how to make gunpowder and established a profitable powder mill. He became an artillery colonel involved in the defense of Boston Harbor. He speculated on shares in the privateer *Speedwell*. He ran a hardware store and a copper-rolling mill. He produced sheet copper for the bottoms of such ships as the *Constitution*. He made false teeth for such hard-bitten clients as General Joseph Warren; in fact after Warren died at the Battle of Bunker Hill, his body was identified through a Revere-made tooth.

And finally, lest anybody say Revere was lazy, he set up a foundry for casting cannon and bells. He became such a talented caster of bells for churches, ships, and public buildings that at least 75 of his best bells are still being rung in New England belfries today and admired for the sweet purity of their tone.

In other words, if there had been no Paul Revere in the Massachusetts Colony, the Town Fathers would have had to invent a dozen or so men to handle his work load.

Yet if it had not been for the poet Henry Wadsworth Longfellow, the history books would have made scant mention of Paul. Long-fellow immortalized him in 1863, by including the narrative poem "Paul Revere's Ride" in his famous *Tales of a Wayside Inn*. True, the poet got several of his facts wrong. But the poem corrected a gross oversight that American historians had been guilty of making ever since the word went out: "Paul!—get on your horse!" Thanks to Longfellow, Revere joined the ranks of such folk heroes as Daniel Boone, Kit Carson, and Davy Crockett.

Church for All People

ON DECEMBER 29, 1723, the Reverend Timothy Cutler climbed into the pulpit of the Old North Church near Boston's bleak Copp's Hill and began giving the first sermon ever heard in that structure. He took his text from the prophet Isaiah: "Mine house shall be called an house of prayer for all people."

It was a modest beginning. Reverend Cutler had no way of fore-seeing that his church would some day become internationally famous for its part in ragging the British and changing world history. Probably his chief concern on that bitterly cold morning was to keep his sermon short and let his parishioners get home early to the warmth of their own firesides.

Regardless, he had unknowingly chosen just the right theme for his homily. Old North did indeed become a house for all people, from privateers to 18th-century aviators. And to a large extent, it remains that way today; it welcomes anybody and everybody.

Officially it was, and is, known as Christ Church. But ask the average Bostonian today where Christ Church is and he'll inquire politely if perhaps you're not in the wrong city. But if you ask him how to get to Old North, he might walk you there himself.

Old North was established as Boston's second Anglican parish, created to serve the overflow from King's Chapel. In fact, it was the

Reverend Samuel Myles, rector of King's Chapel, who laid the cornerstone for Old North on April 15, 1723, with the accompanying exclamation: "May the gates of Hell never prevail against it!"

But though the Anglicans launched the church upon its career, it won the affection of many other sects as the years went by: Irish and Italian Protestants, low-church Episcopalians, Methodists, and French Huguenots, who tried to take it over and make it their own. Even today's Roman Catholics, when parading the statues of their saints through the North End neighborhood, customarily stop at the front door of Old North to serenade the resident vicar and receive his blessing.

In a political sense too, Old North has traditionally been a house for all people. The guest speakers in its pulpit have included such hard-shell political opposites as Calvin Coolidge and Franklin D. Roosevelt. It has benefited by gifts from Yankee sea captains, Honduran mahogany merchants, and King George II. It was King George, incidentally, who contributed Old North's unique Vinegar Bible, in which a typographical error has altered the "Parable of the Vineyard" to the "Parable of the Vinegar." And the church in Revolution days welcomed Tories and Patriots alike, as on those occasions when General Thomas Gage, commanding the British occupation forces during the siege of Boston, would enter his pew (No. 62) at the west end of the left aisle; entering at the east end of the same aisle would be Old North's sexton Robert Newman, the man who hung Paul Revere's signal lanterns in the belfry tower.

In this ecumenical atmosphere, therefore, nobody was surprised one day in 1750 when a 15-year-old Congregationalist named Paul Revere showed up asking permission to form a seven-man guild of Old North bell ringers. Permission was granted, which probably led in time to several good bell contracts for Revere Industries. It also led to some of Revere's offspring joining the Anglican faith and buying a pew of their own (No. 54), which is still occasionally used by Paul's Episcopalian descendants.

It was only logical for Paul to have developed early associations with Old North. The church is just a short stroll from the Revere home and is interesting enough to have been a tourist attraction even in Paul's day, had there been any tourists around.

In Paul's time, the route from home to church would have meant merely walking across a meadow. Today it means turning a corner from North Square to Prince Street and then going up Hanover Street to the Paul Revere Mall.

The Mall is a broad, bricked, semi-enclosed courtyard, dominated at one end by sculptor Cyrus Dallin's statue of Revere on horseback and at the other end by the rising spire of Old North's steeple. Embedded in the surrounding wall are 13 bronze tablets describing incidents in the city's history.

Originally the Mall was part of a pasture owned by one Christopher Stanley, who died in 1646. In his will, he left his land to be used as a site for a free public school, thus becoming the first private benefactor of public education in Boston. Today the Mall is a popular gathering place for North Enders of all ages—for old men who like to sit in the sun and play checkers, chess, or card games; for plump housewives who like to meet and gossip and exchange lasagna recipes; for shoppers who enjoy a chance to sit and rest their aching feet; and for North End youngsters who like to romp and race and go puddle-wading and cadge dimes from tourists. And thousands of tourists following the Freedom Trail walk into the Mall and approach Old North from the rear.

What they've come to see is one of the truly beautiful and storied churches of the world, designed by William Price in the style of Sir Christopher Wren's churches. Its prototype was St. Andrew's-by-the-Wardrobe, which stood in Blackfriars, London, until destroyed by the German Luftwaffe's bombs in 1940.

Fronting on Salem Street, Old North sends its spire rising 190 feet into the air, where it is crowned by a bannerlike weather vane designed by Deacon Shem Drowne, the same artisan who gave Faneuil Hall its unique grasshopper weather vane.

Old North's steeple, incidentally, has had more than its share of ups and downs. It first went into place atop the belfry on August 15, 1740. Blown down by a hurricane on October 9, 1804, it went up again in 1806, this time boasting a new design by Charles Bulfinch. It was brought down for repairs and went right back up both in 1834 and in 1847. It caught fire in 1853 and was put back in shape again in 1855. Again, in 1912 and 1934, it was repaired and restored. Then on August 31, 1954, Hurricane Carol blew it down, and in 1955, it was rebuilt.

Old North's builders are recorded as Messrs. Thomas Tippin

and Thomas Bennett, both of Boston. They did an excellent job. And they had excellent materials to work with.

Their timber came down from the Maine woodlands, from a forest preserve set aside to supply masts for the Royal Navy. The bricks, hand-fashioned, came from a kiln in nearby Medford; and someone, for whatever reason, has researched the useless information that exactly 513,654 of them were used in the building. The church is 70 feet long and 51 feet wide, with walls varying in thickness from 2½ feet to 3½ feet.

Old North's first peal, a set of bells which eventually was rung regularly by Paul Revere and his team of bell ringers, was cast by Abel Rudhall in Gloucester, England, in 1744. The largest of the eight in the peal weighs 1,545 pounds, and the smallest weighs 620.

The organ, built in 1759, has been restored and is still in use. A clock that hangs on the gallery, beneath the organ, was made in 1726 by Richard Avery and Thomas Bennett and is still ticking out the correct time. The statues of the four fat cherubim above the clock were carved in Belgium in 1740 for a French church in Quebec. Before they got to Canada, however, they were seized at sea by the Boston privateer Captain Thomas Gruchy. Being a conscientious Old North parishioner, he brought them home to his vicar, who installed them in 1746.

A bust of George Washington occupies a niche on the Epistle side of the altar, placed there in 1815 as one of the nation's first public memorials to the President. It is such a remarkable likeness that when the Marquis de Lafayette visited Old North in 1824 and saw the bust for the first time, he remarked: "Yes, that is the man I knew, and more like him than any portrait." The niche where the bust sits was originally the window through which the sexton Robert Newman made his hasty exit to escape the British on the night he hung Paul Revere's lanterns in the belfry.

Old North was always a favorite with deepwater New England sea captains, perhaps because they frequently used its spire to get a fix in coastal navigation. At one time, in 1724–30, no less than 20 shipmasters owned pews there.

History tells us that an old Anglican custom of the times called for burying the dead in crypts beneath the church, an act supposedly symbolizing that the deceased parishioners were still members in good standing. Some 1,100 bodies, and probably many more, were interred beneath Old North, where their bones still remain. Among those so entombed were Commodore Samuel Nicholson, the first skipper of the frigate *Constitution,* and the Reverend Timothy Cutler, first rector of the church.

Also buried there was the body of Major John Pitcairn, who commanded six companies on the costly British expedition to Lexington and Concord and who died after stopping a Yankee musket ball at the Battle of Bunker Hill. Years after Pitcairn's burial, Westminster Abbey officials got in touch with Old North, asking that the soldier's remains be exhumed and shipped to London for proper burial there. Records indicate that somebody goofed, intentionally or otherwise— that the wrong bones were disinterred for shipment—and the Major today occupies his original crypt. In any event, Old North continues to display his engraved tombstone where it always has been.

Old North still honors traditions at appropriate times. For example, each year on the eve of April 19, a descendant of Newman or Revere climbs "up the wooden stairs, with stealthy tread, to the belfry chamber overhead" and hangs two lighted lanterns to gleam in the night. And candles in the chandeliers are still lighted for services, as they were for the first time on Christmas in 1724. And each year at Christmastime, a huge lighted tree is placed outside the "Great Window" behind the altar, sending its glow to reflect inside on the pure white walls and galleries.

In a lighter vein in Old North's history was the incident that occurred on September 13, 1757, when a parishioner named John Childs got the jump on the Wright brothers and their flying machine by nearly 150 years. Childs flew from the church's steeple, just as he'd said he would. He did it with homemade wings.

According to the records, Childs gave public notice of exactly what he intended to do. Not many people believed him, but a big crowd gathered in front of the church on Salem Street to see what would happen. John Childs obliged them by flying from the steeple to the ground that September day, and what's more he repeated the performance the next day, not once but twice. As the record of September 15 tells it: "The last time he set off with two pistols loaded, one of which he discharged in his descent; the other missing fire, he cocked and snapped it again before he reached the place prepared to receive him."

At that point, however, Boston officialdom dourly decided that Childs was altogether too much of a distraction to people who should be staying indoors and tending to their business instead of running outside to gawk at the sky. "He is forbid flying any more in the town," they decreed.

Too bad. Old North could have used somebody like the high-flying Childs in making all those repairs to the steeple.

Copp's Hill Reflections

JUST OFF THE FREEDOM TRAIL, only a short walk up the slope from Old North, is the near-perfect place to sit and to reflect upon the strange but lovable traits that have made freedom-conscious Boston unlike any other city in the world. It is called Copp's Hill Burying Ground. It commands a quiet view across Boston Harbor to Bunker Hill Monument and to the home berth of the frigate *Constitution* in the old Charlestown navy yard.

Copp's Hill came into use as a burial ground back in 1660. At that time, King's Chapel Burying Ground was already crowded, and Old Granary was being established to handle the overflow. However, the colonists then dwelling in the North End saw no sense in carting a coffin two miles down the peninsula to the King's Chapel area every time one of their number died. And besides, they were the wealthy and elite of their day. So why shouldn't they have a burial ground of their own? Why go trooping all the way downhill to bury one of their group among the more ordinary colonists?

They answered these questions by setting aside a North End graveyard on pastureland owned by William Copp. And there they began burying their dead neighbors, in ground providing a lovely (if wasted) view of the sea and topped by the first windmill erected in the Bay Colony.

William Copp himself was buried there, which was quite logical. So, in time, were the Reverend Increase Mather, the witch-hunting Reverend Cotton Mather, and the Reverend Samuel Mather. So was Edmund Hartt, builder of the frigate *Constitution*. So was Robert Newman, sexton of the Old North Church. So were hundreds of others, in what eventually became the largest burial ground in the original old Boston.

Among the bodies interred on the hillside was that of one outspoken rebel named Daniel Malcolm, who filed an officially recorded request that his remains be buried ten feet deep so as to be safe from British musket balls. The British reacted to this by using his headstone for target practice, leaving bullet holes that have long since been bored to twice their original size by the probings of curious fingers.

Copp's Hill, particularly on a mild and sunny day, is the ideal place for a man to sit on a grassy tomb and ruminate. There may be others in view, equally lost in their own quiet reflections, but he can be virtually assured that no one will bother him. A Boston cop, stealing time from his beat, may wander in and choose a place on the grass that is a respectful distance from anyone else. A street vendor may leave his pizza pushcart at the gate and stroll down to his own favored thinking spot. A wrinkled old Italian couple may emerge from one of the brick tenement houses nearby, walk across Hull Street to a graveside knoll, and silently sit there gazing eastward toward Palermo. But nobody disturbs anybody else. Copp's Hill seems to have that effect on everyone. It is a particularly good place for thinking about Boston, about the city's idiosyncrasies and its love and respect for freedom.

At the right time of day on Copp's Hill, you may hear the clear, sweet sound of the bells in the tower of Old North Church, just down the slope. Now and then, because of old age and some 200 years of ringing, a bell tone may sound out of pitch. But that takes nothing from the pleasure of hearing the familiar tunes of freedom —"Onward Christian Soldiers," perhaps, or "Battle Hymn of the Republic." Sharp or flat, the message rings true.

And hearing the music, as it drifts out to sea, reminds you that this is the city that once staged probably the loudest and most clamorous musical production ever known to man. Boston may, and does, enjoy worldwide fame for its Boston Symphony Orchestra and

Boston Pops; but there was never anything in the world quite like the Gigantic International Music Festival and World Peace Jubilee of 1872.

If any city cares to duplicate it, the ingredients of the original recipe begin with 100 anvils, 100 hammers, 100 pieces of artillery, and 100 church bells. It builds from there.

The promoters of that GIMF-WPJ extravaganza were Eben Dyer Jordan, who started Boston's Jordan Marsh department store with a piece of red ribbon, and Patrick Sarsfield Gilmore, a bandmaster and cornet virtuoso who had arrived in Boston as a young immigrant from Ireland. Just why they chose to stage the show is still a bit uncertain.

Jordan and Gilmore had produced a big musical fete earlier, in 1869, billing it the National Peace Jubilee. Either the thrill of show business got into their blood, or else they decided people should be glad the Civil War was over, or perhaps they simply assumed that the city deserved an encore. In any event, three years later they raised the curtain on a musical wonder that probably will never be matched.

To do this, they erected a gigantic 50,000-seat music hall near Copley Square. Then they booked a program that would run for 20 days and would fill the coliseum for every performance.

So many glee clubs, soloists, bands, orchestras, choirs, and even barber-shop quartets from all over the nation filed so many entry applications that Gilmore had a chorus of 20,000 voices and thousands of instrumentalists awaiting his baton when he finally got them all assembled for the opening downbeat.

Besides all this American talent, the best bands and the loudest performers in Europe came streaming across the Atlantic to join the party.

Great musical artists were as common as jaywalkers on the streets of Boston that season. Johann Strauss was on hand with his Viennese orchestra, exciting Americans with a popular new rhythm called the waltz. The world's most renowned trumpet player, Herr Saro of Germany, was on hand with the Kaiser's Cornet Quartet from Berlin. France sent its Garde Republicaine Band. London shipped over its Grenadier Guards Band.

For nearly three weeks, then, vast outpourings of music went bounding and echoing up and down the streets of Boston, until the air trembled and most of the pigeons went deaf.

But it was the grand finale that really made musical history. For this event, Gilmore brought his whole aggregation together for two closing numbers that must have shaken the very waters of the Charles River.

One of these presentations was the "Anvil Chorus" from *Il Trovatore,* with 23,000 voices and 2,000 instruments, plus the frantic banging and clanging of 100 anvils, with 100 Boston fire fighters beating out the syncopated rhythm.

The second and final head-splitter was "The Star-Spangled Banner," propelled into orbit by the complete *Il Trovatore* varsity team, augmented by 100 church bells and the thunder of 100 cannon.

Presumably everybody then reeled home for ice-pack treatments. Boston recovered but is not of a mind to repeat the performance.

So go the reveries, as church bells penetrate the quiet surroundings of Copp's Hill. And there are many other stories in the life and freedom of old Boston to reflect upon . . . . .

For example, near this spot in 1639 lived a colonist named Richard Fairbanks, who became the first postmaster in the New World. That was the year when the General Court of the Bay Colony created the country's first official mail system by ruling that "all letters which are brought from beyond the seas, or are to be sent thither" should be left at Fairbanks's home. Richard collected one penny for each letter he forwarded.

Also near this spot, Vikings in their longboats sailed in from the sea, made camp on the shore, and explored inland up the Charles River. And before them, legends say, came monks from Ireland, penetrating the forests to the north. And long before either of them arrived, the ancestors of the early New England Indians were staking out their fish weirs on what is now Boylston Street near Copley Square and trapping giant salmon and sturgeon.

Captain Myles Standish of Plymouth probably passed close to this spot on his yearly trips to northern Maine. The only way he could attend a Catholic Mass was by going north to where he could contact French priests from Canada, and he went there once each year.

And certainly such pirates as Blackbeard and Captain Kidd passed this way many times, for they were frequently in and out of Boston Harbor.

And speaking of brigands, directly below and to the left of Copp's Hill is the spot where eight bandits wearing Halloween masks entered the North Terminal Garage on the night of January 17, 1950, and staged the classic Brink's payroll robbery. They got away with more than $1.5 million in cash, at that time the biggest robbery in American history.

Copp's Hill is also a relaxing place to sit and think of Boston's ghosts. And indeed Boston does have ghosts, real ones. They have been encountered in the walled dungeons of the harbor island forts, in church basements, aboard the frigate *Constitution,* in ancient cemeteries, in kitchens and bedrooms of colonial homes, and in old waterfront warehouses near where the clipper ships used to moor.

But probably the most polite and unobtrusive and generally likable of all the ghosts in Boston's history is the one who spends his time in the Boston Athenaeum library, the ghost of the Reverend Thaddeus Mason Harris. He enjoys the freedom to use the premises, more than 130 years after his death.

Dr. Harris was the beloved pastor of the First Parish Church on Meeting House Hill from 1793 to the time of his retirement in 1836. He was a great scholar and thus became one of the earliest frequenters of the Athenaeum when it was opened in 1807. And from the day he retired to the day of his death in 1842, he spent virtually all of his spare time reading and researching among the library's bookshelves.

Nathaniel Hawthorne was the first to make the acquaintance of the Harris ghost and was so impressed by the experience that he wrote an article about it.

Hawthorne, it seems, had stopped for conversation with a friend on Boston Common one evening in 1842 and was shocked to hear the man remark, "I understand old Dr. Harris is dead."

"Nonsense," Hawthorne protested. "I saw him at the Athenaeum just today."

Nevertheless it was true, as Hawthorne read for himself in the next morning's newspapers. Dr. Harris, it appeared, had died at home several hours before Hawthorne had seen him in the library.

Hawthorne was still further astounded when he visited the Athenaeum again that morning and once again encountered the ghost of Dr. Harris. This time the old gentleman was sitting at a table in the reading room, perusing a newspaper that contained his obituary and the announcement of his funeral arrangements.

Since then, Dr. Harris has returned to the Athenaeum from time to time, never bothering anybody, just quietly going about his ghostly business.

He is still making occasional appearances. Within recent years, a lady visitor from the Back Bay was sitting near the ground-floor book delivery desk one afternoon when she turned to the young librarian on duty and inquired, "Are there ghosts in this library?"

"Certainly," said the librarian. "The ghost of Thaddeus Mason Harris visits here. Why do you ask?"

"Because I believe he just visited me," said the Back Bay lady. "A gentle, elderly man just now rested his hand on my shoulder and then vanished."

The librarian merely nodded. "Of course," he said.

There are many unusual treasures in the Athenaeum, such as books from George Washington's library, the cast of Walt Whitman's massive right hand, and the autobiography of Walton the Highwayman, beautifully bound in his own hide. With these at hand, and looking out the window at Old Granary in an atmosphere that was loved by Longfellow, Emerson, Daniel Webster, and other literary greats, you inevitably succumb to the peace of the place.

That's when you come to understand why Thaddeus Mason Harris keeps returning from the grave. The wonder is not that he likes to revisit the Athenaeum. The surprising thing is that he hasn't introduced his beloved sanctuary to other polite and scholarly ghosts.

Or perhaps he has.....

Spending time on Copp's Hill, reflecting on Boston's past, has a way of making one wonder about such things.

View from the Hill

IN THE MONTHS just prior to the outbreak of fighting in the Revolution, British troops spent considerable time on Copp's Hill and used its strategic location to good advantage. Even today it's easy to see why.

Artillery mounted on the hill could have been brought to bear on the center of Boston to the south, on Charlestown to the northwest, and on any ships in the inner harbor.

Such ships would have had to be French to qualify as targets for the British. The colonials didn't get around to starting a navy until the summer of 1775, when the Massachusetts Colony authorized the outfitting of two armed vessels to serve as privateers. Meanwhile, however, the French had a fleet of exceedingly fine fighting ships that were always ready to take on anything flying the Union Jack.

It would have been much better for British history if, in those days, the U.S.S. *Constitution* had been occupying the spot that is now her home-port berth in the Charlestown section of Boston. That would have placed her within easy reach of artillery fire from Copp's Hill, and she could have been destroyed forthwith. Unfortunately for the British, she hadn't been built yet; she was due to come along later and to run up her best scores against the Royal Navy in the War of 1812.

Probably never in naval history has there been such a love affair between a city and a ship as there is between Boston and the *Constitution*. As the oldest commissioned warship in the world, she is technically subject to United States Navy orders that could send her anywhere from New York to Pearl Harbor. Yet she is as inherent a part of Boston and the Freedom Trail as is Faneuil Hall or King's Chapel. Thus the U.S.S. *Constitution* has been designated an official stop on the Trail. It's too long a hike on foot—2½ miles from Old North Church and across the Charlestown Bridge, but it can be reached by car or special Freedom Trail buses. The Bunker Hill Monument is only a little over a quarter of a mile beyond.

The *Constitution* was born in Boston, built in Boston, blockaded in Boston, and did her best fighting on sorties and voyages out of Boston, and except for one cruise has been docked at Boston since 1897. Three times she was condemned to destruction, and each time she was saved by efforts originating in Boston. In recent years, as many as 700,000 people annually have gone aboard her at her Charlestown berth. And in 1954, Congressman John W. McCormack of Boston fathered legislation in Washington officially designating Boston as the ship's permanent home port. She is as Boston as a pot of beans.

She was built at Edmund Hartt's shipyard, which was overlooked to the northeast by Copp's Hill. She was built 204 feet long, with a 43.5-foot beam. She was made of white oak from Massachusetts and Maine, live oak from Georgia, and yellow pine from Georgia and South Carolina. Her copper sheathing, bolts, and fittings were made by Paul Revere. She draws 23 feet, and in her fighting years, she could cut the waves at 13.5 knots, considerably faster than the Liberty ships of World War II. She was launched on October 21, 1797. She cost $302,718.

Her history has long been a familiar American saga. In 1798, she fought French privateers up and down the East Coast and in the waters of the West Indies. In 1803–1805, it was the *Constitution* against Tripoli and the Barbary pirates. In the War of 1812, her firepower was increased from 44 to 52 guns. Then she proceeded to triumph in battles with the British frigates *Guerrière* and *Java* and in a one-against-two clash with the corvette *Cyane* and the sloop *Levant*. She fought 40 engagements and never lost a fight. She won her nickname *"Old Ironsides"* from the way in which British cannon balls bounced harmlessly off her stout hull.

In 1830, she was saved from the scrap pile by the public's indignation, aroused by Oliver Wendell Holmes's poem, which embarrassed the navy into rebuilding her. In 1905, when the navy planned to use her as a target ship, the Massachusetts Society of the Daughters of 1812 got busy with a restoration fund that saved her life. In the 1920s, when she needed another restoration job, the schoolchildren of Boston started a fund-raising drive that spread to schoolrooms across the nation and produced the money to keep her afloat.

She has needed repairs on several more occasions. But the times are changing; for her latest restoration, the navy requested and Congress authorized a federal appropriation of $4,200,000.

There is no certainty that the Redcoats could have sunk the *Constitution* with cannon fire from Copp's Hill even if she had been around that early. In view of her battle record, *"Old Ironsides"* might well have retaliated by blasting off the top half of the hill all the way back to Boston Common. This we'll never know, which saves face for both sides.

What the British were able to do from Copp's Hill, though, was to hurl cannon fire across the water and into the streets of Charlestown. This they demonstrated during the Battle of Bunker Hill, when Generals Henry Clinton and John Burgoyne used Copp's Hill for an observation site and directed the fire of a British battery of six heavy guns mounted on the slope.

Thousands of spectators, Tory and Patriot alike, crowded onto Copp's Hill for its entertainment value that June day in 1775. The hill provided an excellent view of what was going on across the harbor. The spectators could see the entire show—the noontime naval bombardment by British warships; the ferrying of Redcoats to the Charlestown shore, their uniforms and steel bayonets gleaming in the sun; the pause as American troops behind redoubt and breastworks looked down upon British troops at the base of the slope; the bloody slaughter as the Redcoats again and again marched uphill, fell in swathes, and retreated, only to march grimly up the hill again, until finally the Americans ran out of ammunition and could fight only with fists and clubbed muskets. Copp's Hill provided a great panorama of it all, right up to the last round of fire at five o'clock in the afternoon. The British finally won the day through sheer weight of numbers, although it was a Pyrrhic victory—they lost 89 officers and some 1,000 men.

Today the view from Copp's Hill takes in the Bunker Hill Monument, 221 feet high, standing on Breed's Hill, where the battle actually was fought. The first railroad in America was built in Quincy to haul granite blocks for this monument. Lafayette laid the cornerstone on June 17, 1825, and Daniel Webster gave the oration. Webster was the orator again when the completed monument was dedicated in 1843.

The monument, of course, honors all the victims of the battle but especially General Joseph Warren and Colonel William Prescott, with his classic "Don't fire till you see the whites of their eyes—then aim at their waistbands." Among the artifacts on display at the monument museum is the gun with which a black Patriot named Peter Salem mortally wounded British Major John Pitcairn..

But everything that took place at Breed's Hill on that June day of battle—all of the action viewed from Copp's Hill—came about only as the direct result of a more critical event that had happened two months earlier: gunfire and death at Lexington and Concord.

That April clash was precisely what the long surge toward freedom had been leading to. The time had come to stop talking and begin fighting.

Here Come the British!

THE POET LONGFELLOW, in immortalizing the ride of Paul Revere, noted that events began to get turbulent on the night of April 18, 1775, "just as the moon rose over the bay."

Maybe the moon had something to do with it at that, for it was indeed a crazy sort of night. In Boston, Medford, Lexington, Concord, and seemingly all across the Middlesex countryside, men were abroad and busy long after most respectable farmers had gone to bed.

At ten o'clock that Tuesday night, Revere was summoned in great haste to the Boston home of Dr. Joseph Warren (soon to be General Warren) of the Committee of Safety. As usual, there was a message to be delivered, and Paul was the designated rider.

Warren's information was that some 800 British Grenadiers and Light Infantry troops were assembling on the seaward side of Boston Common, where boats were waiting to ferry them across to Cambridge for the start of a march on Lexington and Concord. It was assumed that the Redcoats planned to capture Sam Adams and John Hancock at Lexington and then move on to Concord to destroy an arsenal of guns and ammunition stored there by the Minutemen. Paul's mission was to beat the Redcoats to Lexington and tell Hancock and Adams to get out of town.

Privately Revere might well have felt irked by the assignment. He had already ridden to Lexington just two days earlier to warn Hancock and Adams that this very operation was in the works and to advise them to start packing. Then Paul had ridden back to Boston and made arrangements for signal lanterns to be hung in the Old North Church to flash the news to Charlestown and beyond when the British made their move—"one if by land and two if by sea." So now again?

Meanwhile, in Lexington that Tuesday night, Hancock was enjoying a date with his fiancée, the beautiful Dorothy Quincy. He and Adams had been staying at the home of the Reverend Jonas Clarke and dividing their time between entertaining Dorothy and swapping yarns around the tables of Buckman's Tavern near Lexington Green. They seemed indifferent to the fact that they were wanted by the British authorities for "offenses of too flagitious a nature to admit of any other consideration than that of condign punishment."

Also abroad that night was young Dr. Samuel Prescott of Concord, who had ridden to Lexington for a date with his girl friend. Still another after-dark horseback rider, William Dawes, Jr., of Boston, was already galloping toward Lexington at Dr. Warren's behest, riding by way of Roxbury Neck to carry the warnings to Adams and Hancock in case Revere failed. And lurking here and there along all the roads from Lexington to Boston were advance groups of mounted Redcoats, determined to intercept and silence any Patriot messengers trying to slip out of Boston. To say the least, there was a lot of action in the countryside.

Withal, on getting his assignment, Revere hustled straight from Dr. Warren's house to the home of Robert Newman on Salem Street and told the Old North Church sexton to put "Operation Lanterns" into effect.

Newman did so, hanging the signal lights in the belfry tower and startling a host of sleepy pigeons in the process. A vestryman named John Pulling cooperated by locking Newman in the church and then hanging the keys on their accustomed hook in Newman's kitchen. The point of this hanky-panky was to fool any Redcoats who might come investigating while Newman was up in the belfry. If the keys were in place, how could there be anybody in the church?

Back in the tower, Newman lit two lanterns as agreed upon. Then he brushed scads of pigeon feathers from his hair and descended to the ground floor, where he exited into history by way of a rear window.

Revere, meanwhile, had gone home to get his favorite riding boots and surtout. Next he called upon two neighbors, Thomas Richardson and Joshua Bentley, and asked them to row him across to Charlestown. On their way to the rowboat, the three men knocked on the door of the Ochterlony-Adan house and asked a friendly Patriot for some clothes to muffle their oars; the response was a petticoat that came fluttering down from an upper window "still warm from the wearer's body."

And so Paul and his companions rowed quietly away from shore, gliding virtually under the guns of the British warship *Somerset* as she swung at anchor on the tide. As Revere later described it, "It was then young flood, the ship was winding, and the moon was rising." That the 8-to-12 watch aboard the *Somerset* missed seeing the rowboat in the moonlight was one of those lucky breaks that occur in normal military operations.

Once ashore in Charlestown, Revere "went to git me a horse." The one he got, "a very good horse," he borrowed from his friend Deacon John Larkin. Larkin didn't know it, but that was the last he'd ever see of that particular animal.

And so began the famous ride. "About 11 o'clock and very pleasant," as Revere later recalled in a letter to the Massachusetts Historical Society.

On leaving Charlestown, Paul was almost picked off by two Redcoats who were hidden in the shadow of a roadside tree. He spurred his horse and outgalloped them both, leaving one rider stuck knee deep in a clay bog. Then he hastened into Medford, where he stopped at the home of Captain Isaac Hall, commanding officer of the local Minutemen.

Besides being a soldier, Hall was also a renowned distiller of Medford rum and most generous in dispensing it. Thus it is worth noting that Paul hadn't bothered to wake up anybody at all between Charlestown and his stop-off at Isaac's. "After that," he later recalled, "I alarmed almost every house till I got to Lexington"—which was around 12:30 in the morning. Perhaps history owes a special nod of recognition to Hall and his midnight rum.

On arriving at Lexington, Revere relaxed for a time in the Clarke house, where he briefed Hancock and Adams on the British troops along the road. Dawes rode up at about one o'clock in the morning and joined the party, whereupon they adjourned to Buckman's Tavern. As Paul put it, "We refreshed ourselves."

Meanwhile, as a result of the alert, Minutemen from farms all around the countryside were beginning to troop into Lexington, toting their muskets and sidearms. Among them came young William Dimond, the official drummer boy of the colonial force, who took up a position in the middle of the Green and proceeded to beat out, over and over again, a "long roll" call to arms. This no doubt awakened what few Lexingtonians were still trying to get some sleep, but it also produced more men for the ranks.

By two o'clock in the morning, some 130 colonial troops were assembled on the Green and were lined up for roll call. Most of them, after logging in, promptly hustled across the way to Buckman's Tavern.

It would have been quite acceptable at this point for both Dawes and Revere to withdraw from the scene of action and go home to bed, since each had completed his assigned mission. By now, however, both men seemed inclined to make a night of it, and there was still the Minutemen's ammunition dump in Concord to worry about. Besides, Buckman's Tavern was getting terribly noisy and overcrowded.

"On to Concord, then?"

"Why not? And we'll wake up everybody along the way."

So off they rode.

At this point in time, Dr. Sam Prescott was finally saying good-night to his girl friend and was about to head home for Concord. Within a matter of minutes, then, he fell in with Dawes and Revere on the highway, all riding in the same direction. This was a break for the two Bostonians and for the cause of freedom, since Prescott personally knew all the families living along the Lexington-Concord road; therefore he could persuade them that Revere and Dawes, with their cries of alarm, were not just kidding around.

But now came trouble. At a spot about halfway between Lexington and Concord, Dawes and Prescott stopped to bang on a farmhouse door to get another Minuteman out of bed, while Revere rode on ahead some 200 yards. Suddenly Paul spotted two British officers waiting in ambush under a tree. He shouted back to Prescott and Dawes, "Here's two of them!"

He was mistaken. There were four of them. And he was surrounded.

In Paul's own words, they "rode up to me, with their pistols in their hands, and said, 'God damn you, stop! If you go an inch farther, you are a dead man!' "

Dawes heard the commotion, leaped on his horse, and galloped off into the darkness. Prescott rushed to aid Revere and tried to beat his way through the blockade with his riding whip. The Redcoats easily outmaneuvered both men and ordered them to stand still or have their brains blown out. Then they forced Revere and Prescott into a nearby pasture for interrogation.

"Put on!" yelled Prescott and promptly jumped his horse over a stone wall and disappeared in the direction of Concord. Revere took advantage of the confusion to spur his horse toward a near-by clump of trees. But it just wasn't Paul's night. When he got to the trees, he discovered six more mounted Redcoats waiting for him there. They took up where the others had left off, making him dismount at pistol point. And then the questioning began.

"Where are you from?"

"Boston."

"What time did you leave there?"

"Eleven o'clock."

"Sir, may I crave your name?"

"My name is Revere."

"What—Paul Revere?"

Sometimes it's nice to be recognized; sometimes not.

Paul willingly told them what he'd been doing all night and warned them that there'd be at least 500 angry Minutemen coming along the road at any moment. They topped this lie of his by telling him that there were at least 1,500 British regulars on their way, also due at any moment.

At this stage of the standoff, an officious British major galloped up, put his pistol to Paul's head, and took over the interrogation, asking all the same questions that Paul had just answered. Finally they put Paul back on his horse and led him off in the direction of Lexington.

They were within about a half-mile of the Lexington Meeting House when they heard a gunshot.

"That's just to arouse the countryside," Paul explained.

The party halted, hesitated, and then moved on. A few minutes later, they heard a volley of musketry. It was enough to start the Redcoats worrying.

"Dismount," the British major told Paul. "We're going back to Cambridge. Leave your horse with us and be on your way."

And that was the last ever seen of Deacon Larkin's steed.

Left alone, Paul cut across a cemetery and a pasture or two and made his way back to the Clarke house. There he reported his experience to Hancock and Adams and advised them to leave town immediately. They agreed this was a good idea and decided to head for nearby Woburn. After traveling two miles, they asked Paul to return to Buckman's Tavern with a friend and get a trunk of papers belonging to Hancock.

By now it was 4:30 in the morning. The Minutemen had left the tavern and were drawn up in two ranks on the Lexington Green, awaiting the orders of Captain John Parker. Coming down the road were the Redcoats, six companies under the command of Major John Pitcairn.

"While we were getting the trunk," says Revere's report, "we saw the British very near, upon a full march. We hurried toward Mr. Clarke's house. On our way, we made haste and passed through our own militia, who were on the Green behind the Meeting House, to the number of about 50 or 60. It was then daylight.

"I passed through them, and as I passed I heard the Commanding Officer say words to the effect 'Let the troops pass by and do not molest them without they begin first.'

"When the British troops appeared in sight behind the Meeting

House, they made a short halt. One gun was fired. I heard the report, turned my head and saw smoke in front of the troops. They immediately gave a great shout, ran a few paces, and then all fired.

"I could first distinguish irregular firing, which I supposed was the advance guard, and then platoons. At this time I could not see our militia, for they were hidden from me by a house.

"The British troops appeared on both sides of the Meeting House. In their front was an officer on horseback. I heard a continual roar of musketry. Then we made off with the trunk."

And so the war began, touched off by a volley of lead from Pitcairn's regulars. The Patriots returned fire raggedly and then broke, leaving on the Lexington Green eight Minutemen dead and ten wounded.

As the British regrouped their column for the march to Concord, the drummer boy Dimond threw his drum over a stone wall and picked up the musket of a dead Minuteman. Then he too set out for Concord, taking a shortcut through the woods to get there ahead of the Redcoats.

The battle that day at the old North Bridge over the Concord River was, of course, quite a different story. By the time Pitcairn's troops reached the Concord River, Minutemen were streaming in from all directions—from the towns and villages of Bedford, Lincoln, Carlisle, Acton, Chelmsford, Littleton, Weston, Sudbury, Reading, Billerica. By noon, both sides were trading heavy fire at the bridge. The Redcoats, outnumbered two to one, were forced to retire. Then began their terrible retreat toward Boston, with the Minutemen harassing them with deadly fire, picking off the colorfully uniformed British regulars from behind every rock, fence, and building along the way. Nor did the arrival at Lexington of British reinforcements change the pattern.

Finally, with the King's troops back on Charlestown Common and under the protection of British naval guns, the day's fighting came to an end. The Minutemen could do no more; they dispersed and trudged home to their families.

Hours earlier, upon hearing the first gunfire at Lexington Green, Sam Adams had cried, "What a glorious morning is this!"

Glorious for some, terrible for others. The American losses were 49 dead, 39 wounded, and 5 missing. The British figures were 73 dead, 174 wounded, and 26 missing.

It was only the beginning. But it was a guarantee of victory to come. From that day on, freedom was inevitable. Its achievement has stirred the hearts of men and women everywhere.

And so too the Freedom Trail was inevitable. Its significance has reached out to places and people far beyond Salem Street and Old South and Griffin's Wharf. It is recognized wherever men rebel against tyranny, as they always shall.

Index

Adams, John, 92
  quoted, 90
Adams, Samuel, 16, 30,
  32, 47, 60, 70, 92,
  113, 146, 147, 149,
  151
  quoted, 32–3, 71, 152
Alcott, Louisa May, 35
Alden, John (father), 80
Alden, John (son), 80–1
Alden, Priscilla, 80
Allerton, Isaac, 29
"America," 39
American Board of Com-
  missioners for For-
  eign Missions, 38
American Education So-
  ciety, 38
American Missionary As-
  sociation, 38
American Temperance
  Society, 38
Ancient and Honorable
  Artillery Company
  of Massachusetts,
  18–19, 53, 87, 115
Andros, Lady, 52
Andros, Sir Edmund, 48–
  9, 52, 68, 88
Anglicans. See Church of
  England

Annapolis, Maryland, 70
Anne, queen of England,
  49–50
Arthur, Chester Alan,
  115
Athenaeum library. See
  Boston Athenaeum
Atlantic Monthly, 63
Attucks, Crispus, 47, 91,
  92
Autocrat of the Breakfast
  Table, The, 31
Avery, Richard, 133

Bank, William, 125
  quoted, 124
Banks, Nathaniel, 33
Banner, Peter, 38
Bay Colony, 25, 52, 66.
  See also Puritans
  and Ancient and Hon-
  orable Artillery
  Company, 53, 87,
  115
burying grounds. See
  Copp's Hill Bury-
  ing Ground; Gra-
  nary Burying
  Ground; King's

Chapel Burying
  Ground
charters of, 22, 80
crime and punishment,
  20, 39–40, 52, 84,
  87. See also Witch
  trials
daily life in, 56–9, 85
divorce in, 84
education in, 54–6, 59,
  60. See also Bos-
  ton Public Latin
  School; Harvard
  University
emergence of social
  classes, 57, 58, 59
founding, 21–2
housing in, 56–7, 57
marriage ceremonies in,
  84
postal system, 139
printing and publishing
  in, 47, 59–60
religion in, 20–1, 21–2,
  39, 42, 44, 55. See
  also Congregation-
  alists; Episcopa-
  lians; Puritanism;
  Quakers; Roman
  Catholics; Uni-
  tarians

Bay Colony (*cont.*)
  religious festival in,
    44–5
  slavery in, 43, 44
  welfare system in, 57–8
  witch trials. *See* Witch
    trials
  "woman's rights," 83–
    5
  work laws, 58
Beacon Hill, 30, 31, 33,
    34–6, 93, 122, 123
Benjamin Franklin's
  Birthplace, Site of,
    60, 66
Benjamin Franklin
  Statue, 60
Bennett, Thomas, 132–3
Bentley, Joshua, 148
Bible: and witch trials,
    74
Bishop, Bridget, 77
Blackbeard, 139
Blackstone, William, 17,
    18, 18–20, 24
Board of Customs Com-
    missioners, 90
Book of Common Prayer,
    50–1
Booth, Edwin, 35
Boston, 16, 31, 70. *See
    also* Freedom Trail
Back Bay, 31, 65
Brink's payroll robbery,
    139–40
Charlestown section of.
    See Charlestown
Chinatown, 15
colonial Boston. *See*
    Bay Colony
founding of, 54
and international music
    festival, 137–9
literary heritage of, 63–
    4
North End, 44, 122–
    3, 126, 131, 132
old street names, 120–
    1
printing and publish-
    ing, 63
Roxbury section of,
    13, 17
South End, 44–5
Boston Antiquarian Club,
    94
Boston Athenaeum, 140–1

Boston Common, 15–16,
    16, 17–20, 22–4, 47,
    52, 76, 123, 146
Boston Common Council,
    94
Boston Harbor, 31, 69,
    70
Bostonian Society, 94
Boston Massacre, 69–70,
    90–2
  broadside quoted, 116–
    19
  Paul Revere's engrav-
    ings on, 116, 127
Boston Massacre Site, 92
Boston Pops, 137–8
Boston Public Latin
  School, 54, 59, 60
Boston Stone, 123
Boston Symphony Or-
  chestra, 35, 137
Boston Tea Party, 16,
    70–1, 113
commemorative plaque,
    72
*Boston Weekly News-
  Letter:* quoted, 89
Boydell, John, 23
Bradford, William, 25,
    26, 27, 28
  journal quoted, 26, 27,
    28, 29
  Of Plimoth Plantation,
    32
Brandeis, Louis, 35
Brattle, Thomas, 50
Breed's Hill, 145. *See al-
  so* Bunker Hill, Bat-
  tle of
"Brimstone Corner," 16,
    37–8
British East India Com-
  pany, 70
Buckman's Tavern (in
  Lexington), 147,
    149, 151
Bulfinch, Charles, 30, 31,
    33, 113, 132
Bulfinch, Thomas, 50
Bunker Hill, Battle of,
    128, 134, 144
Bunker Hill Monument,
    136, 143, 145
Burgoyne, John, 71–2,
    144
Burroughs, George, 77,
    78

Cabot, Frederick Picker-
  ing, 35
Calef, Robert, 82–3
Cambridge, 146
Caner, Henry, 50
Capen, Hopestill and
  Patience, 121
Capen, Thomas, 121
Carrier, Martha, 77–8
Carroll, Paul Revere,
    114
Central Burying Ground,
    17
Charles River, 31
Charleston, South Caro-
  lina, 70
Charlestown, 136, 142,
    143, 144, 147, 148,
    149, 152
Chatham, 12, 13
Chicago, Illinois, 93
Childs, John, 134–5
Chilton, Mary, 53
Christ Church. *See* Old
  North Church
Church of England, 22,
    48, 51, 84
Clarke, Jonas, 147
Clinton, Henry, 144
Codman, John, 43
Common, the. *See* Boston
  Common
Conant, Roger, 21
Concord: battle at, 145,
    152
Concord River, 152
Congregationalists, 38,
    48. *See also* Puri-
  tanism; Puritans
  and Congregational
    Church, 22, 40, 66
Constitution, 128, 133,
    136, 137, 140, 142–4
Constitution of 1780
  (Massachusetts), 32
Continental Army, 123
  Massachusetts' contri-
    bution to, 124–5
Coolidge, Calvin, 65–6,
    67, 115, 131
  quoted, 65–6
Copp, William, 136–7
Copp's Hill, 31, 130,
    137, 139, 140, 142,
    143, 144, 145
Copp's Hill Burying
  Ground, 136–7

Corey, Giles, 77, 78–9
Corey, Martha, 77
Cotton, John, 53
Courser, William, 122
"Cradle of Liberty." *See* Faneuil Hall
Crease, Thomas, 62–3
Curley, James Michael, 60–2
Cutler, Timothy, 130, 134

Dallin, Cyrus, 132
Danbury, Connecticut, 61
Dartmouth, 70
Davenport, James, 122
Dawes, William, Jr., 52–3, 147, 149, 150
Declaration of Independence, 92
signers of, 47
d'Estaing, Count, 51
Dimond, William, 149, 152
Dorchester Company of Adventurers, 21
Drowne, Shem, 114, 132
Dyer, Mary, 23, 43

Ebenezer Hancock House, 122
Elizabeth I, queen of England, 74
Emerson, Ralph Waldo, 24, 114
Endicott, John, 21, 25, 29
Episcopalians, 51. *See also* Church of England

Fairbanks, Richard, 139
Faneuil, Andrew, 111–12
Faneuil, Peter, 23, 47, 49, 111–13
quoted, 112–13
Faneuil Hall, 16, 70, 111, 112–13, 115, 119
grasshopper weather vane, 114–15, 132
as news center, 115–16:
broadsides quoted, 116–18
Fields, James T., 63

First Parish Church, 140
Fleet, Thomas, 47
Fort Hill, 31
Fox, George, 42
quoted, 42
Franklin, Benjamin, 16, 47, 60, 66, 68, 122
birthplace, site of, 60, 66
statue of, 60
Franklin, James, 60
Franklin, Mr. and Mrs. Josiah, 47
Freedom Trail
landmarks nearby. *See* Boston Athenaeum; Boston Stone; Bunker Hill Monument; Copp's Hill Burying Ground; Ebenezer Hancock House; Paul Revere Mall
length of, 17, 143
official sites, 16. *See also* Benjamin Franklin's Birthplace, Site of; Benjamin Franklin Statue; Boston Common; Boston Massacre Site; Boston Public Latin School; *Constitution;* Faneuil Hall; Granary Burying Ground; King's Chapel; Old Corner Book Store; Old North Church; Old South Meeting House; Old State House; Park Street Church; Paul Revere House; State House
origin of, 11
starting point, 16, 17
Freeman, James, 50–1
Frog Pond, 20

Gage, Thomas, 131
Gallows Hill (in Salem), 77, 78
Gardner, Thomas, 21

Garrison, William Lloyd, 39
General Court (Massachusetts state legislature), 30, 43, 58, 59, 59–60, 139
Charter of 1650, 55
George II, king of England, 131
George III, king of England, 31, 50, 70–1
Gigantic International Music Festival and World Peace Jubilee of 1872, 137–9
Gilmore, Patrick Sarsfield, 138–9
Gloucester, 21
Glover, Goodwife, 76
Goelet, Francis: journal quoted, 89
Golden dome: of State House, 30, 33, 36
Golden Dome (pub), 36, 37
Gompers, Samuel, 65
Good, Sarah, 77
Goodwin, Mr. and Mrs. John, 76
Goose, Mary. *See* "Mother Goose"
Gordon, George A., 67
quoted, 67, 68
Government Center (in Boston), 60
Granary Burying Ground, 16, 46, 47–8, 136
Grasshopper weather vane (on Faneuil Hall), 114, 132
theft of, 114–15
Great Fire of 1872 (in Boston), 72
Greenough, Richard S., 60
Gresham, Sir Thomas, 114
Griffin's Wharf (in Boston Harbor): and Boston Tea Party, 70, 71
Gruchy, Thomas, 133

Hale, John, 79
Hall, Isaac, 148–9

Hall of Flags, in State House, 30, 34
Hancock, Ebenezer, 121–2, 122
Hancock, John, 30, 31, 32, 47, 60, 70–1, 92–3, 112, 113, 121, 122–3, 146–7, 149, 151
Harris, Thaddeus Mason, 140–1
Harrison, Peter, 49, 52
Hartt, Edmund, 137, 143
Harvard, John, 54
Harvard Divinity School, 50
Harvard University, 54–5, 60, 67, 73
Hawthorne, Nathaniel, 35, 140
Hibbins, Anne, 75
Hill, The. See Beacon Hill
Holmes, Oliver Wendell, 35, 35–6, 144
quoted, 19, 31
Hopkins, Matthew, 74
House of Representatives (Massachusetts), 34, 51. See also Massachusetts state legislature
Howe, Julia Ward, 35
Howes, Tom, 12–13
Huguenots, 111
Hutchinson, Anne, 41–2, 62, 75
Hynes, John B., 11

Innocent VIII, Pope, 74
Inquisition: and witch trials, 74–5

Jackson, Andrew, 23–4
James I, king of England, 74
James II, king of England, 48, 49, 80
James, Henry, 35
quoted, 35, 38
Jesuits, 42, 44
persecutions of, 44
Joan of Arc, 74

Johnson, Sir Isaac, 46–7
Jones, Margaret, 75
Jordan, Eben Dyer, 138
Jordan Marsh department store, 62, 138
Joy, John, 35

Keayne, Robert, 52–3, 87–8, 88, 115
Kennedy, John F., 115
Kidd, Captain, 88, 139
King's Chapel, 48, 49–52, 130–1
St. Sauveur monument, 51, 52
King's Chapel Burying Ground, 46–7, 52–3, 136

Lafayette, Marquis de, 145
quoted, 133
Larkin, John, 148, 151
Latin School. See Boston Public Latin School
Leddra, William, 23
Lewis, Mercy, 76–7, 78
Lexington
battle at, 145, 149, 151–2, 152
Paul Revere's ride to, 128, 146–9
Lexington Meeting House, 151
Lincoln, Amos, 33
Longfellow, Henry Wadsworth
and Paul Revere's ride, 128–9, 146
quoted, 69
Louis XIV, king of France, 111
Louis Philippe, king of France, 122

McCormack, John W., 143
MacDonald, Donald, 114
Malcolm, Daniel, 137
Massachusetts Bay Colony. See Bay Colony
Massachusetts Bay Company: charter of, 32

Massachusetts Colony, 44, 70, 80, 142. See also Bay Colony
Massachusetts Historical Society, 148
Massachusetts Society of the Daughters of 1812, 144
Massachusetts Spy, 121
Massachusetts state legislature, 34, 41, 51, 52, 54. See also General Court
Mather, Cotton, 75–6, 82–3, 137
exorcism of witches, 81–2
quoted, 66, 84
and witch trials, 73–4, 76, 77, 78
Mather, Increase, 75, 80, 82, 137
Mather, Mrs. Increase, 81
Mather, Samuel, 137
Medford, 146, 148
Merrymount settlement, 25–9
Minutemen, 146–7, 148, 149, 150, 151, 152
Monroe, James, 33, 115
Morison, Samuel Eliot, 20–1, 35
defines Puritanism, 20–1
Morton, Thomas, 26–9
quoted, 27, 28
"Mother Goose," 16, 47
Myles, Samuel, 131
quoted, 131

National Capitol: and Charles Bulfinch, 33
National Peace Jubilee, 138
Naumkeag, 21. See also Salem
New England Company, 21
New England Courant, 60
Newland, Jeremiah: verses quoted, 119
Newman, Robert, 131, 133, 137, 147

New York City, 70
Nicholson, Samuel, 134
Nickerson, William, 12–14
Norton, John, 66
Norton, Mary, 66
Nurse, Rebecca, 77

Of Plimoth Plantation, 32
Old City Hall (Boston), 60, 62
Old Corner Book Store, 62, 63–4
Old Granary. *See* Granary Burying Ground
"*Old Ironsides,*" 143–4. See also *Constitution*
Old North Church, 16, 130–2, 132–5, 147
Old South Church, 38. *See also* Old South Meeting House
Old South Meeting House, 16, 48–9, 65–70, 70–2
and Boston Tea Party, 70–1, 72
Old State House, 31, 34, 86–7, 89, 93–4, 123
Osburn, Sarah, 77
Otis, James, 16, 47, 90

Paine, Robert Treat, 47
Palmer, Edward, 87
Parker, John, 151
Parkman Bandstand, 18
Park Street Church, 16, 37, 38, 39
Parris, Samuel, 76, 78
Paulist Fathers Center and Chapel, 37
Paul Revere House, 126–7
Paul Revere Mall, 132
"Paul Revere's Ride," 128–9
Pennsylvania, 44
Philadelphia, Pennsylvania, 70
Phillips, Henry, 23
Phips, Lady, 79, 80
Phips, Sir William, 79–80, 83

Pilgrims, 26, 29, 54
and Puritans compared, 54
Pitcairn, John, 134, 145, 151, 152
Plymouth, 13, 21, 25, 26, 27, 28, 29, 54
founding of, 54
religion in, 21
Plymouth Colony Court, 13
Pope Day, 44
Prescott, Samuel, 147, 149–50
Prescott, William, 145
Price, William, 132
Prince, Thomas, 68–9
Prison Reform Society, 38
Providence, Rhode Island, 41
Pulling, John, 147–8
Puritanism, 20, 22, 39–40
defined, 20–1
dissenters, attitude toward, 21, 41–2, 49
persecutions under, 22–3, 42–4
Puritan Pronaos, The, 20
Puritans, 21, 48, 49, 56. *See also* Bay Colony
daily life of, 56–9, 85
and education, 54–6
and Pilgrims compared, 54
and welfare system, 56–7
Putnam, Ann, 76–7, 78, 83

Quakers, 20, 42–4
persecution of, 22–3, 42–4
Quincy, 49, 145
Quincy, Dorothy, 147
Quincy, Josiah, 92

Ratcliffe, Robert, 48
Rehoboth, 17
Revere, Paul, 16, 30, 32, 47, 52–3, 116, 126, 127–9, 133, 143
"midnight" ride of, 128–9, 146–52

and Old North Church
lanterns, 16, 131, 133, 134, 147
quoted, 32–3, 148, 149, 150, 151–2
and State House, 33
statue of, 132
Revere, Mrs. Paul, 126
Revoire, Apollos de, 128
Revolutionary War, 72, 92, 131, 153. *See also* Bunker Hill; Concord; Lexington
events leading up to, 47, 69–70, 90, 113. *See also* Boston Massacre; Boston Tea Party
navy, 142
Treaty of Paris, 93
Rhode Island and Providence Plantations (colony), 41
Richardson, Ebenezer, 116
Richardson, Thomas, 148
Robinson, William, 22–3
Roman Catholics, 20, 37. *See also* Jesuits
and King's Chapel, 51–2
persecution of, 44, 51
Roosevelt, Franklin D., 53, 131
Royal Exchange (in London), 114
Rudhall, Abel, 133
Rule, Margaret, 81–3

Sacred Cod of Massachusetts, 34, 114
St. Andrew's-by-the-Wardrobe (in London), 132
St. Bride's (in London), 38
St. Sauveur, Chevalier de, 51, 52
monument to, 51, 52
Salem, 21, 40, 40–1
witch trials, 67, 73, 74, 76–7: death roster in 1692, 77
Salem, Peter, 145
Saltonstall, Nathaniel, 79
Sargent, John Singer, 35

Scollay Square, 11
Seider, Christopher, 116, 127
Sewall, Samuel, 40, 67
diary quoted, 40, 88
and witch trials, 67–8, 73, 79: apology quoted, 67
Shawmut, 19. *See also* Boston Common
Silence Dogood, 60. *See also* Franklin, Benjamin
Smart, Thomas, 23
Somerset, 148
Somerset Club, 35
Stamp Act, 69, 90, 113
Standish, Myles, 12, 27, 28–9, 139
Stanley, Christopher, 132
State House, 16, 30–1, 31–4, 36, 93, 122
as history museum, 32
Stevenson, Marmaduke, 22–3
Stoddard, Thomas, 121
Story of Massachusetts, The: on Thomas Morton, 26
Strauss, Johann, 138
Sugar Act, 69, 90
Sumner, Increase, 93

Tales of a Wayside Inn, 129
Thatcher, Thomas, 66
Thomas, Isaiah, 121
Ticknor, William, 63
Tilley, John, 21
Tippin, Thomas, 132–3

Town House (Boston), 87–8, 92. *See also* Old State House
Town Library (Boston), 87, 88
Townshend Acts, 70, 90
Treaty of Paris, 93
Trimountain, 31. *See also* Boston

Union Club, 37
Union Oyster House, 121, 122
Unitarians, 38, 51
U.S.S. *Constitution.* See *Constitution*

Van Buren, Martin, 23–4
Vergoose, Isaac, 47
Vinegar Bible, 131

Ward, Nathaniel: quoted, 58–9
War of 1812, 32
Constitution's role in, 142, 143
Warren, Joseph, 128, 145, 146, 147
Washington, George, 52, 72, 93, 113, 122, 123, 141
memorial to, 133
Webster, Daniel, 35, 145
quoted, 124–5
White, John, 21
Willard, Samuel, 66–7, 68
William and Mary, British monarchs, 49

William III, king of England, 80
Williams, Jonathan, 70
Williams, Roger, 40–1, 43
Winthrop, John, 21–2, 52, 66
quoted, 22
Witchcraft, 73, 74–5, 75–6, 77, 78, 81–2, 83
exorcism of witches, 82
Witch trials
biblical basis for, 74
and Cotton Mather, 73–4, 76, 78
in Europe, 74–5
executions, 20, 74, 75, 77, 78, 78–9
under the Inquisition, 74–5
in New England colonies, 73–4, 75, 76, 77–9, 80–1, 83: death sentence decreed, 75; Salem, 73–4, 76–9
Wollaston, 25. *See also* Merrymount settlement
Wollaston, Captain, 25–6, 26
Woodbridge, Benjamin, 23
Wren, Sir Christopher, 38, 68, 132
Writs of Assistance, 47, 90

Yarmouth, 12
Young, Alse, 75